# Worcester people and places, past and present

First published in Great Britain in 2012
David Field
Gaillet Press
29 Perdiswell Street, Worcester
Worcestershire WR3 7HZ

Designed and produced by Leysfield House Limited, Worcester.
2012 photography by Tania Field.
Printed in England by S S Media Limited, Rickmansworth, Hertfordshire.

ISBN  978  0  9522408  3  9

# Worcester

## people and places, past and present

a personal collection
by Dave Field

Gaillet
Press

**ACKNOWLEDGMENTS**

Much of my research was through delving through
various books and archives, I am indebted to the
following:
Worcester Library and History Centre
*Forgotten Worcester* H A Leicester
*Worcestershire* F T S Houghton
*A Survey of Worcester* Valentine Green, 1764
*Berrows Worcester Journal*
*The Worcester News*
The Worcester Library and History Library
I also thank the Wikipedia: The Free Encyclopedia,
and Wikimedia Commons.
The writing of this book has brought me into
contact with so many others, but too many name,
who deserve my acknowledgement, thank you.

# Contents

Foreword **6**

Chapter 1    Past history  **7**

Chapter 2    Historical trivia  **13**

Chapter 3    Interesting buildings, monuments, parks, etc.  **27**

Chapter 4    Worcester streets  **81**

Chapter 5    Interesting people of Worcester, some famous,  **93**
             some not so famous

Chapter 6    Historical titbits  **149**

Chapter 7    Places around Worcester  **157**

# Foreword

I was born in Minster Union Workhouse on 20 December 1929. It was the year after my mother entered the establishment, that workhouses were abolished, many being renamed 'Public Assistance Institutions' continuing to care for the elderly, infirm and destitute. Uniforms were abolished and more freedom was allowed with 'inmates' being called residents. Nevertheless, these workhouses will never lose their stigma. Finding it impossible to get work, and with me to look after, my mother literally dumped me, at the age of three months, on the steps of Dr. Barnardo's Homes, as it was called then, at Stepney Causeway in the east end of London.

After a childhood spent moving around several foster homes, I ran away to London during World War II, and thereafter lived most of my life in the big city. Over the years I started, and cultivated, an interest in history and people.

Whilst I was living in Cheshunt, Hertfordshire, I satisfied my interest in local history by writing and publishing a book called *Cheshunt: Its people past and present*. In 2006, I moved to Worcester and the love of local history was reignited. Within just a few months I was writing yet another book: *Worcester people and places, past and present* I just love writing about people; given the chance I will listen to them talking about themselves for hours. The world is changing so rapidly, and the past should be captured and recorded.

I sincerely hope that you will enjoy reading this book, just as much as I enjoyed researching and writing it.

David Field 2012

# Chapter one
# Past history

### A brief look at early life in Worcester

Before the Romans came to this area the Britons had cleared away a large portion of thick wooded area away from the banks of the River Severn, in order to create some sort of stronghold, and it is this very site where the city of Worcester stands today.

Roman coins found in Worcester, reproduced from 'A Survey of Worcester', Valentine Green, 1764

The Romans invaded Britain in 43AD. Roman legions built a road on the east bank of the River Severn between the legionary forces of Kingsholm and Wroxter which are on the River Severn near Shrewsbury. This Roman road passed through Worcester (possibly Castle Street to Broad Street).

When the Romans finally departed England in 410AD, there were conflicts between the Saxon army, the Picts and Scots, who quickly retired further north, thus allowing the Saxons to settle permanently on British soil. This created seven Saxon kingdoms, one of which was Mercia, of which Worcester was a part.

The parish of Worcester came into existence around 700AD. Becoming a place of importance, a modest church was erected by Bishop Saxulph, which stood on part of the grounds of the present Worcester Cathedral which was built in 983.

In mediaeval times the population of Worcester was around 10,000, today the population of Worcester has increased to over 95,000.

### Sheriff Urso
*Urso d'Abitot, Sheriff of Worcestershire*

Urso of Worcester, as he is styled in Domesday, was a Norman, a mediaeval Sheriff of Worcester and royal official under Kings William I, William II and Henry I. A native of Normandy, he came to England shortly after the Norman Conquest of England, and was appointed Sheriff of Worcestershire in about 1069. He held a lot of land in Worcestershire, as well as land in Herefordshire, Warwickshire, and Gloucestershire; as a landlord he was notoriously evil. He became the most powerful layman in Worcester. Sheriff Urso built a castle in Worcester, none of it remains today, but the castle's outer bailey encroached on the cemetery for the monks of the Worcester Cathedral Chapter, earning the Sheriff a curse from the Archbishop of York.

## Worcester Chronicle

The Anglo-Saxon Chronicle is a collection of annals, by year, in Anglo-Saxon language (Old English), which records the history of the Anglo-Saxons. Originally compiled on the orders of King Alfred the Great in approximately A.D. 890, and subsequently copied and distributed around the country. These were maintained and added to by generations of anonymous scribes until the middle of the 12th Century.

Nine of those manuscripts survive, the Worcester Chronicle being one of them.

We like to think of this document as the ultimate timeline of British history from its beginnings up to the end of the reign of King Stephen in 1154.

Worcester was attacked many times in the civil war (in 1139, 1150 and in 1151) between King Stephen and Empress Matilda, who was the daughter of King Henry I.

## Battle of 1088

This battle was chronicled by 'Florence of Worcester,' who served under Wulstan, Bishop of Worcester. His Latin manuscripts have survived to this very day. They record the following:

'Bernard de Newmarket. Roger de Lacy, who had just marched against the King at Hereford, Ralph de Mortimer, all of them conspirators, with the men of Earl Roger of Shrewsbury, having assembled a great army of English, Normans and Welshmen, made an inroad into the province of Worcester, declaring they would burn the city, spoil its cathedral church and take heavy vengeance on the local inhabitants. On hearing this Wulstan, a man of great piety and dove-like simplicity, one beloved by God and the people whom he ruled in all things, constant and faithful to the king as his earthly lord, was exceedingly troubled but soon recovering confidence prepared himself to stand by his people and his city.

The garrison and the whole of the citizens assembled , declaring they would meet the enemy on the other side of the Severn.'

'Being armed and ready, they met the Bishop on the way to the castle who said: 'Go, my children, go in peace, go in security with the blessing of god and mine. Trusting in the Lord, I promise you this day no sword shall injure you. Be firm in your allegiance to the king, manfully fighting for the safety of the city.' With these words they crossed the bridge and beheld the enemy approaching rapidly at a distance. Among them already raged the madness of war for, despising the commands of the Bishop, they had burnt many portions of his territory. When he heard this, the Bishop was stricken with great sorrow, beholding the destruction of the property of the church and, taking counsel, launched against them a heavy anathema.

A wonderful thing, proclaiming most clearly the power of God and the goodness of man, came to pass, for immediately the enemy, who were wandering scattered over the fields became stricken with so great a weakness in their limbs and enfeebled by such a blindness of the outward eye that they were hardly able to bear their arms. They could neither recognise their friends nor distinguish those who were attacking them from the opposite party.

*While blindness deceived them, confidence in God and the Bishop's benediction comforted our men. So stupefied were the enemy that they knew not how to escape, neither did they seek any means of defence but fell an easy prey. The footmen were slain, the horsemen captured – English, Normans and Welshmen – the rest just escaping by a feeble flight. Those who were faithful to the King, along with the household of the Bishop, joyfully exulting, returned without loss to their own homes, thanking God for the safety of the property of the church and thanking the Bishop for the wholesomeness of his counsel.'*

## Charles II and Oliver Cromwell

The future King Charles II (right) brought an army of around 12,000 men to Worcester in August 1651, having marched 300 miles in just three weeks from Scotland.

This was known as the 'Battle of Worcester,' when Charles tried to reclaim both crown and country from the Parliamentarians, who were led by Oliver Cromwell (left). This was to be the last battle on English soil, Charles was defeated in fields near the village of Powick, on the 3rd of September, 1651. Because of its loyalty to the King, Worcester was given the title of 'The Faithful City.' 'Fidelis Civitas' is incorporated in the city's coat of arms.

## Walled City of Worcester

Worcester was a walled city with 7 fortified gates:

1. Bridge Gate (once known as Water Gate)
2. Foregate
3. Friars Gate
4. Saint Martin's Gate
5. Sidbury Gate
6. Frog Gate and
7. Priory Gate.

In the 1640s these walls were in a terrible state and were not capable of withstanding a siege. Even the seven gates were in very poor condition. However, new fortifications were set up, the most important of which was Fort Royal.

## Worcester's early streets

During the reign of Philip and Mary (1555–56), the following streets were designated for the sale of various produce, thus:

| | |
|---|---|
| Broad Street *cattle* | Queen Street *corn* |
| Edgar Street *horses* | Church Street *crockery* |
| Angel Street *sheep* | Saint Nicholas Street *vegetables* |
| Dolday *pigs* | The Cross and High Street *meat* |
| Saint Swithin's Street *poultry* | Fish Street *fish* |
| Mealcheapen Street *meal* | |

When the Market House was built in 1804, all these markets were forbidden, and the sale of all these products had to come from the designated shops, or in enclosed areas.

## Worcester City Charters

Worcester is supposed to have been originally built and fortified by the Britons, later occupied by the Romans and considerably enlarged under the Saxons, who gave it the name of Weorganceaster. A strong wall at one time encircled it, remains of which still exist. It became the seat of a bishop in 680. Its growth and prosperity were much checked by the continual inroads of the Welsh. Nevertheless it was a place of importance at the time of the Norman conquest.

It suffered severely during the reign of John from the incursions of its old foes, was often besieged, and several times captured and pillaged.

Royal City Charters have been granted by a monarch to a group of citizens in order to bestow certain privileges upon them. It would have given the city certain rights to act independently from the shire and to make decisions regarding its governance in its own right. Worcester city holds seventeen Charters:

| | |
|---|---|
| Richard I  12 November 1189 | Henry VI  11 June 1423 |
| Henry III  17 March 1227 | Edward IV  20 December 1461 |
| Henry III  23 February 1256 | Henry VII  5 February 1486 |
| Edward III  12 July 1330 | Philip and Mary  12 April 1555 |
| Edward III  2 April 1377 | Elizabeth I  20 May 1559 |
| Richard II  1 April 1378 | James I  2 October 1622 |
| Richard II  29 March 1396 | James II  18 February 1685 |
| Henry IV  4 December 1403 | Elizabeth II  15 May 1974 |
| Henry V  12 December 1413 | |

With the charter of James I, it became a city and county of itself, and was governed by a mayor and corporation. In 1835, under the Municipal Reform Act, the city was divided into five wards, and is now governed by a mayor, 12 aldermen, and 36 councillors. It was at the request of the bishop, in the reign of King Alfred, that a burgh (derived from the word burh, meaning 'fortified town') was to be built at Worcester. The first incorporation charter (sometimes referred to as the Certificate of Incorporation – primary rules governing corporation) was granted by Philip and Mary in 1554, but in 1622, James I made the City a separate county and granted a corporation of a common council, consisting of 24 citizens, that included the mayor and aldermen; plus another body of 48, who elected the mayor from among it's 24 councilmen; this is when the '48' of the Corporation of Worcester was established.

## Local stone quarries

Worcester is mainly a city of brick and timber. There are very few stone buildings; reason being that local stone quarries such as those that were in Ombersley, were a variety of various coloured red and greeny-grey sandstone. Very easy to cut and carve, but very much prone to the weather, that's the reason why the cathedral is continually undergoing restoration work.

## River Severn floods

The River Severn broke its banks in 1672, creating a massive flood, a brass plate on the wall at Watergate, on the river's pathway close to Worcester Cathedral, shows the height of that flood. There are 19 plaques recording flood marks at Watergate (from 1672 to 2007). Other notable floods were in: 1770 (highest at 15.65m), 1811, 1847 and 1914.

Historians also mention a tremendous flood in 1484. This flood carried away men, women and children. It was called the Duke of Buckingham's water, because he lay with an army, ready to march against Richard III. and was stopped by it. The floodwater from the River Severn came so suddenly that many roads were flooded, making the movement of his soldiers impossible.

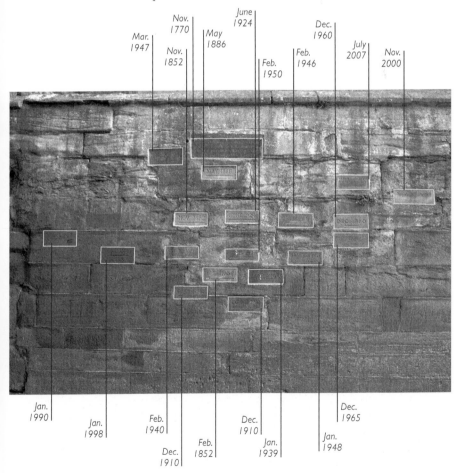

Mar. 1947 | Nov. 1770 | Nov. 1852 | May 1886 | June 1924 | Feb. 1950 | Dec. 1960 | Feb. 1946 | July 2007 | Nov. 2000

Jan. 1990 | Jan. 1998 | Feb. 1940 | Dec. 1910 | Feb. 1852 | Dec. 1910 | Jan. 1939 | Dec. 1965 | Jan. 1948

Beside the entrance to the Watergate leading to College Green, by Worcester Cathedral some of the flood levels have been marked on the wall. The highest in living memory was the flood of March 1947, the mark for this flood on the extreme left and is around one foot higher than the 2007 flood. The larger plaque at the top marks the highest known flood of 1770.

*Above: Flooding at the swan sanctuary, by Worcester Bridge, south side, July 2007*

*Below: Rescuing residents from the houses along the river in Waterworks Road, July 2007*

# Chapter two
# Historical trivia

## Belisha beacons

These beacons with their distinctive striped poles and orange lit globes were named after Leslie Hore-Belisha (1895–1957), Minister of Transport, who introduced them in 1934.

Belisha Beacons arrived in Worcester in 1936. Zebra crossings were first used in 1951, and appeared in Worcester one year later.

## Berrow's Worcester Journal

This newspaper, formerly the Worcester Postman, was established in 1690. It is the world's oldest continually published newspaper. Stephen Bryan became the first editor of this newspaper in 1709. The Worcester Postman was sold for 2d. over a wide area of the Midlands.

In 1730, the paper changed its name to the Weekly Worcester Journal when it started printing local news.

In 1748, the paper passed into the ownership of Harvey Berrow, becoming Berrow's Worcester Journal.

One remarkable story reported by Berrow's Journal, in March, 1918, was the display on the Cathedral Green, of a captured German bi-plane.

On the 10th June 2008, Prince Charles met the editor, John Wilson, at the Commandery during his royal visit to Worcester. Mr Wilson said:

*'Receiving the royal seal of approval was a proud day for the paper. It has been part of the Faithful City for more than 300 years and it was an honour for its role in the community to be recognised...'*

*'In 1911, Berrow's Worcester Journal reported that thirteen-year-old Archibald Henry Beven of Summer Street, had been charged with stealing a bicycle, valued at £1 10s. He was given six strokes of the birch.'*

## Blockhouse

The Blockhouse was a name given to fields outside Saint Martin's Gate and Friar's Gate; where there were fortifications to 'block' the Cromwellian army from access to the City.

## Bridge across the Severn

The first bridge across the Severn was made of wood, in 1299 a fire in Tybridge Street destroyed the bridge and many houses. A new bridge was built in stone in 1313.

A group of country gentry headed by the Earl of Coventry, invited John Gwynn, R.A., to build the Severn Bridge in 1769. The Earl of Coventry laid the foundation stone on July 24,1771. A few months later there was a major flood and it was realised that the arches of the bridge would be too low. John Gwynn redesigned them almost three feet higher.

The bridge took ten years to complete and was opened in September, 1781.

Worcester Bridge was substantially widened and encased in new stonework in 1931.

## Canals

The Midlands was a crucial hub for Britain's canals during the Industrial Revolution. James Brindley, a master canal engineer, built the first canal, the Manchester and Bridgewater Canal in 1759, and continued across the country into the Midlands.

Here are some of those canals:
The Grand Union Canal
Shropshire Union Canal
Trent & Mersey Canal
Staffordshire & Worcester Canal
Worcester & Birmingham Canal
Macclesfield Canal.

The Birmingham Canal linking the City of Birmingham to the Staffordshire and Worcester Canal, was completed in 1815.

The Worcester and Birmingham Canal links the two cities, and was built to connect the River Severn in Worcester to the Birmingham Canal System via a quicker route than the Staffordshire and Worcestershire Canal. The Staffordshire and Worcestershire Canal, leaves the River Severn at Stourport.

The Worcester and Birmingham Canal is well known for its 58 locks, climbing to 428 feet from the level of the River Severn in Worcester up to Birmingham.

## Canal restoration 2011

This restoration programme has restored 12km of waterways which links the Droitwich Canals with the River Severn at Hawford. At Droitwich it links with the Worcester and Birmingham Canal. Twelve locks were restored and four new locks were added.

The scheme opens two links: the Droitwich Barge Canal, from the River Severn at Hawford to Vines Park in Droitwich Spa; and the Droitwich Junction Canal, from Vines Park to the Worcester & Birmingham Canal at Hanbury Wharf, both were abandoned in 1939.

## Charles I and II, and the Civil War

This story has been told so many times in so many books that I decided to stick to the points of interest. Beginning with the execution of King Charles I at Whitehall on January 30, 1649. At the time, Charles II, only 18 years of age, was living in the Hague. On hearing of his father's death, Charles allowed himself to be called King of England, and on February 15th, that same year, the Scottish Royalists were proclaiming Charles II as King of Great Britain, France and Ireland.

After the execution of Charles I his head was stitched back on. He was first buried in a lead coffin at Saint James House, then later re-buried at Windsor Castle. The exact location was unknown until 1813, when workman found the body of Charles I during reconstruction work at the castle.

Montrose, in Scotland, was ready and willing to help. Ormond, in Ireland, (who became Lord Lieutenant of Ireland in 1644) was also willing to support the King. And so, Charles took a very decisive step, appointing Montrose as Lieutenant-Governor of Scotland, Captain-General of all forces raised in Scotland and those out of England and Ireland.

Marching from Scotland to Worcester, Charles was facing the 'New Model Army' commanded by Oliver Cromwell. This turned out to be the last battle of the Civil War, fought out in the fields around the City of Worcester on September 3, 1651.

*Armour, helmets and pikestaffs sculpture on the canal bridge at Sidbury, adjacent to The Commandery, the Royalists' headquarters*

The Battle of Worcester was between a Scottish army, supported by a few English Royalists and led by Charles II, and the Parliamentarian army that was commanded by Oliver Cromwell. As nightfall set in, on that September day, the King's forces were in full retreat along Worcester's winding streets.

Charles fled out of the back door of his lodgings, and rode off, just as the Parliamentary troops arrived at the front of the mansion. Charles then began his famous six-week escape to France. He rode through the fields with Lord Wilmot; along a new path (now called Sansome Walk) to Barbourne Brook, where they paused to consider which road to take. They chose the Ombersley route and headed over the River Severn.

On September 6th, parliament put up a £1,000 reward for his capture.

During his escape to France, Charles had the occasion to disguise himself as a maid, or as a woodcutter.

Charles and one of his loyal officers, William Carlis, were forced to leave their hideout to sit in the branches of a large oak tree near Boscobel House, Staffordshire.

Lord Grenville's inscription which is on a stone adjoining the Boscobel Oak at Dropmore reads:

*'This tree, raised from an acorn of the oak which sheltered Charles II at Boscobel, is planted and cherished here as a Memorial, not of his preservation, but of the re-establishment of the Ancient and Free Monarchy of England, the true source of Prosperity and Glory.'*

Charles II lived in France, later moving to Holland where he stayed in exile.

A report in the Worcester News on 25 April, 2007, stated, that: 'those Battle of Worcester enthusiasts, were trying to sort out fact from fiction'.

Members of the Battle of Worcester Society, who met earlier that year were very keen to celebrate the anniversary of the 1651 Civil War clash. But in order to do that, they wanted to separate historical fact from local legend.

Battle of Worcester Society Secretary, Bernard Mills, was quoted as saying:

*'We don't want to disavow stories, but we want to unearth the historical facts. There are no records of any mass graves during the Civil War, but there are rumours of there being one at Powick.*

*Why should Worcester have been an exception? We want people to help us unearth the reliable historical archives out there that would shed light on the battle.'*

I was told that there's a burial pit very close to the Cathedral. It's said to be under College Yard, the site of the Chapel of the Charnal House.

There is a sub-basement beneath number 10 College Yard, where part of the arch of the chapel protrudes from the floor. It was opened up in 1941; giving access to the chapel which was seen to be crammed almost to the ceiling with skeletons, plus traces of lime that had been scattered over them.

Oliver's Mound in Shrawley Woods, near Worcester, could well be associated with this Civil War, because it is not only the site of an ancient castle, but could also be a burial site for many of the Royalist and Parliamentarian soldiers who died in the battle.

When Oliver Cromwell died in 1658, his son Richard Cromwell took over. Arguments arose among many powerful figures, as to whether Richard had the ability to rule. It was now the time when the restoration of the monarchy was to take place. A letter was sent to the exiled King Charles inviting him to come home. On May 29, 1660, the day of his birthday, the King was to be seen in a great ceremonial dress, entering London.

This day was to become 'Oak Apple Day' in honour of a tree that protected King Charles. But in 1859, it ceased to become a public holiday (though it still survives to this day at the Royal Hospital Chelsea via Chelsea Pensioners).

## Diana visits Worcester

It was in May, 1992, when Diana visited Worcester. That was the time when the 'People's Princess' dressed in a delightful pink outfit, officially opened the Rose Hill home of Saint Richard's Hospice. Sadly five years later the Princess was dead.

## Diglis Basin, Worcester

Diglis Basin has undergone a major development. Where once the great Royal Worcester Porcelain factory stood, there is now an estate of modern apartment blocks surrounding the boat moorings. But Diglis Basin still has some fine old buildings, a boat chandlery shop, and its own canal 'pub,' the Anchor Inn. A very friendly inn with a lovely atmosphere; I know, because I've been there several times with my German Shepherd dog, Ellie.

During the winter of 2002 Diglis Basin was completely drained of water when British Waterways workers hit an 18th century unmarked storm sewer. They were making improvements to the mooring facilities. Boats were left stranded in the thick mud, British Waterways' staff worked hard to move more than thirty boats with wood or fibre-glass bottoms, that would have been damaged if they had been left in the mud.

Jonathan Green, from British Waterways, said 'it was like someone had pulled the plug out of a basin, with the water gushing down the hole.'

## Discover history with Paul and Helen

'The Worcester Story Tour' is a ninety-minute historical walking tour with two costumed guides (Paul and Helen).

Paul Harding takes the group on a short tour of the city centre. He runs through the history of the city, from Roman times to the modern day. I decided to go on this tour, and here is just part of the commentary that Paul gave:

'We'll take you around parts of Worcester and if you've got any questions on what I'm referring to, then I'll do my best to answer them. We'll start here at the Guildhall because there are a few things that I'd like to point out to you.'

'We are not going to look at just buildings that are present today, but I'll use archeological facts that were here prior to what has been built. This will give you a good understanding how Worcester has developed up to the present day.

The Guildhall dates back to 1721. We believe the architect was Thomas White. He did produce some of the carvings here, but what we don't know is whether he designed the whole of the building.

When looking at the accounts of Thomas White, we discover that if he did design the whole building he must have done it at a very cheap rate. His accounts don't quite tally up to what it should have cost. However, there's some interesting points about this building. For example, Thomas White's signature mark. It was a snail, if you look very carefully you'll spot it in the

frieze over the window, left of the main door.

When they put the lift entrance in the North Wing they found the mediaeval foundations of an earlier building, and because of the size of the sandstone foundations we know that this building, which we believe to have been a three-storey one, was of some substantial size and much further forward than this one. So, in the 1400s there would have been quite an enormous timber-framed building.

Although this is the Town Hall, it has always been called the Guildhall, because this is where all the guilds met in earlier days. Very few towns have retained the name, York is one.

There are statues of Charles I and Charles II either side of and guarding the front door.

*A statue of Queen Anne is over the doorway, because the architecture of the building is in the Queen Anne style (the statue was originally on a separate plinth in the forecourt). The wings of the building were added on later. When this Guildhall was rebuilt, it was no longer used as a guildhall but took on the role of county and city court. Here in the north wing was installed the judges lodgings.'*

*The south wing is now the Tourist Office of Information, it was at one time a coffee shop.*

*Most of the buildings in the High Street may look Georgian, but if you look over the road you will see, for example, what was once the Golden Lion Pub, is now the Coffee Republic. It has a Georgian frontage, but if you look inside its a typical timber-framed Tudor building, that has a brick frontage. Most of the timber-framed Tudor buildings in Worcester have been treated this way... this area used to be called Lychgate Shopping Centre because here once stood the entrance to the Cathedral.'*

### Elizabeth's visit to Worcester in 1575

It was during a slump in the cloth trade (with 5,000 people out of work as a result of it), that Queen Elizabeth I visited Worcester in 1575. Her visit raised the hearts of the people.

It was during this visit, that the City of Worcester acquired its second coat of

arms. While the Queen was touring the city, she spotted a pear tree which had been planted especially for her, in Forgate. It was laden with black pears, and pleased the Queen so much, and she bade the City to add to the emblem three black pears to its coat of arms.

### Fire

It was on June 19, 1113, that the city of Worcester was consumed by fire; even the buildings inside the castle, as well as the Cathedral could not escape this horrendous fire.

According to the Worcester Annals, one monk and twenty inhabitants perished.

Then, in November, 1233, another huge fire burnt down part of the city; and the Cathedral was once again badly damaged.

### Floods: water, water, everywhere

The weekend of July 20, 2007 was a shocker, with the worst flood in living memory. Large areas of Worcestershire were cut off. Torrential rain battered the heart of England on the Friday night, flood waters trapped 10,000 motorists on the M5 which had to be closed most of the night.

A motorist was found drowned in his Volvo in 12 feet of floodwater. Another man was driving home from work, he phoned his wife to say the force of water was dragging his car off the road near Drakes Broughton. That weekend:

- *Parts of Worcestershire were under six feet of water.*

- *500,000 people were without water, power or homes.*

- *Tens of thousands of families were put on red alert as rivers reached levels not seen for more than fifty years.*

- *350,000 people in Gloucestershire were without running water, when a treatment plant flooded.*

- *A hundred people were forced to sleep at emergency centres.*

- *Stretches of the M5, A44, A42, A420 A419, A417 and the A4095, were closed.*

- *All buses from Worcester stopped running because the bus station was flooded out.*

- *Upton-upon-Severn was cut off. The Army took in food and medical supplies by boats and helicopters.*

- *The RNLI was called out to help rescue people from homes.*

- *Severn Bridge at Worcester was closed to both traffic and pedestrians on the Saturday.*

- *People in the Severn View Hotel were trapped, the ground floor was flooded.*

- *Rising flood water caused vast numbers of fish to colonise in flooded areas on Pitchcroft. Environment officials and council wardens had the unenviable task of rescuing trapped fish, and were commended for saving over 10,000 fish.*

## Flood defence

It was announced that the Environment Agency had given the green light to a £765,000 flood defence programme at Powick in 2009. Work began that year on a permanent flood barrier behind the houses on the A449. The project is being paid for through local levy funding, with contributions from Worcestershire County Council's highways department, the Powick Parish Council and village fundraising activities.

## Green Badge Guides

The Green Badge Guides are made up of ten local people who truly love their city, and are interested in bringing the Worcester City's local knowledge to all its visitors. To do this, the Green Badge Guides will take the visitor on a short walk around the city streets, recounting some fascinating tales about famous or infamous characters, who helped to create the city we know today.

## Hanging (execution)

In 1809, eleven men were sentenced on the same day, at the Worcester Assizes held at the Guildhall.

The unlucky prisoners were:

Benjamin Jones for housebreaking.
Joseph Nobbs, convicted of housebreaking.
Samuel Pain for stealing money.
William Huffal for sheep stealing.
Sampson Jones also for sheep stealing.
John Cotton for sheep stealing.
William Nicholls for sheep stealing.
John Maggott for sheep stealing.
William Watkins for sheep stealing.
John Lane and brother Richard, convicted of killing their uncle, Thomas Good.

## Headless body under the Cathedral

The well-preserved skeleton of a man was excavated, in 1987, from the base of Worcester Cathedral's south-east tower – a place normally reserved for royalty, senior godbrothers or the very rich. Cardiff scientists produced an amazing 8-page report on their findings, revealing that the skeleton was over 500 years old. The body was wearing knee-length leather boots suggesting that he had died with his boots on. These, and fragments of twill-weave worsted clothes the pilgrim wore, helped them to identify the body.

The pilgrim's wooden staff, found alongside his body, had a pierced cockle shell tied to the top, reminiscent of the scallop shell tokens associated with the shrine of St James of Compostela, in north-west Spain, a most important pilgrim destination, after Jerusalem and Rome during the Middle Ages. The head and neck of the skeleton were missing due to the construction of a wall through the pilgrim's grave during Victorian restoration work. This was Britain's first ever discovery of a grave with a clothed pilgrim, complete with staff.

The headless body was reburied in 1999, the grave is marked just north-west of the quire steps in the Cathedral. The staff and his long boots are on display in the crypt.

## King Charles House

The most important house in the City of Worcester stands in New Street. It was originally called Berkeley Mansion, and had three storeys. A fire destroyed the top floor, as well as the corner of the house near the Cornmarket. Rowland Berkeley and his wife Catherine, lived at Berkeley Mansion for 34 years. They had seven sons and nine daughters. The family moved during the Civil War; and rented the

FROM THIS HOUSE
KING CHARLES II
ESCAPED
HIS ENEMIES
AFTER THE BATTLE
OF WORCESTER
SEPTEMBER 3
1651

house out to Mr Durant who was acting host to King Charles II; the house becoming the King's headquarters in 1651.

## Leofric of Mercia

Leofric had become Earl of Mercia by the 1030s. This made him one of the most powerful men in the land. Harthacnut, King of England at the time, made himself unpopular with heavy taxation during his short reign. Two of Leofric's tax-collectors were killed at Worcester by angry locals. The king was so enraged by this that in 1041 he ordered Leofric to plunder,

*King Edward the Confessor and Earl Leofric of Mercia see the face of Christ appear in the Eucharist wafer*

burn and lay waste the whole city. This command must have tested Leofric, Worcester was the cathedral city of the Hwicce, who were his people. According to the Chronicler of Worcester, Leofric of Mercia died 'at a good age' in 1057. He was the husband of the famous Lady Godiva who rode naked through Coventry in protest at his tax plans.

## Lych Gates

Entrances to churches had a 'Lych Gate' (Lych is a Saxon word for a corpse), which took the form of a table with a roof to protect the coffin from the weather. In mediaeval times when a person died, they were taken to the churchyard and placed on this table and the priest would cover the body with a special shroud which was the symbolic removal of any bad traits of the deceased. The priest would then conduct the first part of the funeral service under this temporary shelter.

## Market House

Opposite the Guildhall once stood the Market House which was opened in the early 1800s. This is an extract form the book 'A general history of Worcester' by John Chambers, 1820.

*The Market House is situate facing the guildhall, in the High-street, to which it is highly ornamental. with stone arched Its front entrance is of stone rustics, with a principal arched opening, supported by tuscan columns over which is a panneled square pedement, in which are the city's arms, ornamented with trophies. On each side of the principal archway are two smaller entrances, one to the fish (established 1811), the other to the butchers' stands. In the year*

*1800, the back of the King's Head Inn, once the scene of theatrical fame, was purchased for a market place, and the present building, designed by the late Mr. Richard Morton, was opened Feb. 1804…*

## Mercian Regiment

On 5 September 2007, residents watched a day-long ceremony, plus a civic reception with the Mayor of Worcester, Stephen Inman, as the newly-formed local regiment displayed its new uniform and cap badge. This regiment had been formed by the merger of three infantry regiments:

**The Worcestershire and Sherwood Foresters Regiment**
**The 22nd (Cheshire) Regiment**
**The Staffordshire Regiment**
**The West Midlands Regiment and**
**The King's Cheshire Regiment.**

## Nelson comes to town

When the battle-scarred naval chief, Admiral Lord Nelson made his entry into Worcester on a beautiful summer's day in 1802, he got a great welcome. After a short tour of the city in his carriage, through a flag-waving throng, he arrived at the Hop Pole Hotel in Foregate Street. Edward Gill records:

*'Men, women and children looked out from upstairs windows and every available vantage point along the route, to get a good view of the carriage bearing the hero, wearing a glittering assortment of medals and decorations. He was drawn along the main streets through a surging sea of flag-waving citizens.'*

## Population growth

In 1801, the population of Worcester was 12,909. A census in 1921, revealed that the population of Worcester had grown to 48,848; and by 2001, the population had increased to 93,358. Today the population of Worcester is approximately 95,000.

## Prince of Wales' visit to Worcester

October 28, 1932 was one of the most exciting and momentous days in the City's history. It was the day when the Prince of Wales (later to be Edward VIII) came to officially open the newly widened and re-constructed Worcester Bridge; the new Cripplegate Park; a Nurses' Home; and the opening of the newly-extended Royal Infirmary.

At the Guildhall, Mayoress, Miss Diana Ogilvy, gave the Prince a book-bound Address of Welcome. This visit lasted six hours.

## Railway accidents, Worcester line

In 1840, two people were killed when the boiler of a railway engine burst in Bromsgrove station.

The following year a stoker had both legs cut off by an engine in a cutting at Bredon.

In 1843 a drunken porter lay down across the railway line, just outside Worcester station, to enjoy a sleep, and was decapitated by a train.

Then in 1859, a curious accident occurred in one of the Worcester thoroughfares, when Richard Groves stooped down to pick up an object; it exploded, severely injuring his eye. The object turned out to be a fog signal which had fallen off a railway cart. The Worcester and Wolverhampton Railway Company were held responsible.

## Railway bridge across the Severn

The first railway bridge across the Severn was built in 1860, by the firm of Stephen Ballard of Colwall, backed by Thomas Brassey, who was a great railway constructor. In 1904, the arched spans were replaced by a new girder bridge, designed by J C Ingles, the GWR Chief Engineer of the time.

## River Severn

The Severn is the longest river in Great Britain, at 220 miles, flowing from Plynlimon, high in the Welsh mountains, down to the sea in the Bristol Channel.

It's a very dangerous river, claiming well over 400 lives. It has the second highest tide as anywhere else in the world, a range in excess of 50 feet.

The River Severn gets its name from a mythical story concerning the drowning of the nymph, Sabrina. Sabrina was originally from the Welsh name Habren, then became Hafren, later translated to the English name Sabren then Sabrina. Here is a version of that mythical story:

*'The three sisters (who were water nymphs who loved the sea) met in the Black Mountains to discuss how they might wend their way down to the sea.*

*The first sister, Ystwith, took the most direct route and was the first to reach the sea.*

*The second sister, Varga, with a loving taste for the beautiful landscape took the route through hills and valleys and became the River Wye.*

*The third sister, Sabrina, took a 180-mile route along the Severn and drowned in the river.'*

## Sabrina statue

The Sabrina Statue by W Calder Marshall R.A., is at the City Art Gallery. John Milton, the poet, introduces Sabrina, the nymph of the River Severn thus:

*'There is a gentle nymph not far from hence, That with moist curb sways the smooth Severn stream,*

Sabrina, being thrown into the Severn, Worcester City Art Gallery & Museum

*Sabrina is her name, a virgin pure.'*

The legend of Sabrina comes from Welsh traditions of the 12th century. It tells how, on the death of the famous Brutus of Troy, known as the founder and first king of Britain. The dominions would be divided into three parts:

*Brutus of Troy's eldest son, Locrinus, taking the chief part (England).*

*His second son eldest son, Camber, taking the West part (Wales).*

*The youngest son, Albanactus, taking the North part (Scotland).*

The Huns, under King Humber invaded the country and Albanactus was killed; his people driven into the protection of Locrinus, who managed to defeat the invaders. King Humber was drowned in a river, today called River Humber.

Among the spoils of Locrine's victory over the Huns, was the beautiful Hunnish Princess Estrildis, with whom Locrine fell in love. The fact that he was already engaged to be married to Guendolen, the daughter of Corineus, made very little difference to him. This situation caused a scandal.

Corineus was outraged. He attacked Locrine with an axe, forcing Locrine to do justice to his daughter, with the result that they were married straight away.

Locrine's love for Princess Estrildis remained strong and for seven years he kept her hidden at his palace. There she bore him a daughter, named Sabrina. At the same time Guendolen had given birth to his son, named Madan.

When Corineus died, Locrine divorced his wife, Guendolen; acknowledged Estrildis and her daughter Sabrina. Guendolen took revenge and together with her Cornish people, went to war against Locrine; he was slain in battle. Guendolen commanded that Sabrina and her mother be thrown into the river. To this day that river is called in the British tongue, 'Sabern' (corruption of the latin word Sabrina). Today as the Severn.

## Schools merge

**RGS** WORCESTER

RGS (Royal Grammar School) and the Alice Ottley School, both in Upper Tything, merged together in 2007, to become 'RGS Worcester and The Alice Ottley School. Neither school wanted to relinquish their historical name. The Royal Grammar School in particular, has a Royal Charter.

Most of the school buildings were paid for by Charles William Dyson Perrins, grandson of William Perrins, creator of the original Lea & Perrins Worcestershire sauce. Charles was an 'old boy' and a member of the school's governing body. The name has reverted to its original name: RGS Worcester.

### Soldiers come home to Worcester

In December, 2009, thousands of people lined the streets of Worcester to welcome home men of the 2nd Battalion the Mercian Regiment (Worcester and Foresters) after their tour of duty in Afghanistan.

A service took place at Worcester Cathedral, just before the parade, to remember the five Mercians who lost their lives in Afghanistan. One of those men of the 2nd Battalion the Mercian Regiment being Private Jason Williams from Worcester.

### Theatre Royal

In 1904, the Theatre Royal in Angel Street, underwent a dramatic internal face-lift. The Worcester Journal of that year reported the following:

*'Those who now visit the theatre will find the interior transformed in a manner most pleasing to the eye, by the display of a number of very beautifully coloured frescoes adding greatly to the appearance of the upper portions of the house… The frescoes are the work of Mr Louis F. Silas who is a specialist in this direction and who has*

*been occupied for several months in completing this commission. Subjects placed on the ceiling represent the Muses and are executed in the French style. Over the proscenium are two large figure subjects representing Tragedy and Comedy. The colouring generally is very fine, and the entire effect will be regarded generally as most artistic.'*

### Toilets

In September 2005, Worcester City Council cut down the number of public toilets in the city from seven to five, in order to save money. One toilet in Quay Street, closed for three years, was put up for sale for £100,000 in 2007. It was sold for £86,000 in 2008, to a city architect, Adrian Hull, and turned into offices.

### Trams – horse-drawn to electric

Public transport consisted of horse-drawn trams in 1881. The Worcester Electric Traction Company Ltd. brought open-top trams to Worcester in 1903, the lines used by the horse-drawn trams, were dug up and new ones installed, together with overhead power cables.

The trams served Barbourne, Astwood

Cemetery via Rainbow Hill, Shrub Hill Railway Station, London Road and Saint John's.

## Worcester Coat of Arms

In 1634 the castle coat was registered, together with the coat bearing three black pears, for the Worcester Coat of Arms,.

Legend has it that the Worcester archers rallied under the pear trees before the battle and thus the pear blossom was worn as a badge by the Worcestershire Yeomanry Calvary from the beginning of this century, up until 1956.
The motto translates:
*'The City faithful in war and in peace.'*

## Worcestershire Regiment

The Worcestershire Regiment dates back to 1694. It was formed by an officer of the Coldstream Guards, Colonel Thomas Farrington, who was raising a new regiment in London. During that time it was customary for a new regiment to be named after its colonel; and up until 1751 this regiment had eight different colonels, thus it had eight different names.

In 1751 regiments were given numbers, and this regiment was No 29.

Worcester Cathedral has very close links with the Worcestershire Regiment. The Regiment's Colours rested in Saint George's chapel, Worcester Cathedral, whilst the Regiment was on active service. Many tributes to its past soldiers can be seen in the Cathedral.

## Worcestershire Sauce

Worcestershire Sauce was first made at 68 Broad Street, by two dispensing chemists,

John Wheely Lea and William Henry Perrins. The Lea & Perrins brand was put on the market in 1837. It has been produced at the Midlands Road factory since 1897. HP Foods took over the business in 1930, though subsequently acquired by other groups including Group Danone.

H J Heinz Company purchased the business in 2005, and continue to manufacture the original 'Lea & Perrins Worcestershire Sauce' under the name of Lea & Perrins, Inc.

Recently, after more than 170 years, the original recipe of Worcester sauce was revealed. The recipe was discovered by Brian Keogh's daughter, Bonnie Clifford, who found the notes, that went on display at the Worcester Museum in 2009.

Brian Keogh, who was a former Lea & Perrins accountant, found the recipe in two leather-bound folios, written by hand in sepia ink, in a skip outside the Midlands Road sauce factory where he worked. Mr Keogh, who retired in 1991, found rough encoded notes about the recipe's secret ingredients, believed to date back to the mid-1800s.

Mr Keogh, author of a book called 'The Secret Sauce', avidly collected memorabilia connected with Lea & Perrins, before he died in 2006, aged 80.

## Worcestershire Yeomanry

In 1794, the Worcestershire Yeomanry, also known as The Queen's own Worcestershire Hussars, was formed at the outbreak of the Napoleonic Wars. As part-time soldiers, and they were to serve within the British Isles against French invaders or at troublesome internal issues of unrest. They were to serve as garrisons in both Britain and Ireland to deter revolts and free up regular troops for foreign service. Their commanding officer was Lieutenant Colonel John Somers Cocks, the first Lord of Eastnor Castle. His son served as Aide-de-Camp to the Duke of Wellington.

A member of the Worcestershire Yeomanry, Edwin Hughes, was a survivor of the charge of the Light Brigade.

The Yeomanry disbanded in 1827 due to lack of service, saving a military expense. The Regiment was to be reformed four years later to suppress serious unrest in the area which had started the year before and culminated into the Worcester Riots of 1831 and 1832. The Worcestershire Yeomanry saw a lot of service, in the 1830s and 1840s against striking workers mostly from Lord Dudley's mines or factories. Lord Dudley was a fabulously wealthy local dignitary, in fact one of the richest men in the world, and coincidentally Colonel of the Yeomanry. He financed the Regiment, and obviously made them work for their pay to his own gain.

## Worcester Yeomanry Cavalry (WYC)

A 'living history unit' based today in Worcester, is a re-enactment group of military history enthusiasts is dedicated to recreating the Worcestershire Yeomanry formed at the height of the Napoleonic Wars. WYC pay exceptional detail to recreating the original uniform, weapons and civilian costumes from the period; the helmets they wear, are exact copies of the originals held by Worcester City Museum. The group perform re-enactments at various venues throughout the year, including at Eastnor Castle.

## Worcester Ships

1. The **S.S. Worcester** traded with Europe via the River Severn until 1853 made her first voyage in 1850 from Oporto.

2. **HMS Worcester (I)** (right) a training ship for the merchant navy cadets between 1862 to 1876 on the River Thames.

3. In 1876, a two-decked ship called the

Frederick William, on loan from the Admiralty, replaced the smaller training ship, and renamed HMS Worcester (II). During World War II this Worcester was used as a training base by the Royal Navy, but by 1945 was in poor condition and was moved to Thurrock, but cheated the shipbreakers by sinking at her moorings, having broken her back.

4. A replacement ship was found in the form of the **Exmouth** whose war years were spent at Scarpa Flow. This ship, built in 1904, of steel and iron, was to become the third and last **Worcester (III)** training ship, redesigned to accommodate 750 ratings.

# Chapter three
# Interesting buildings, monuments, parks, etc.

## Alice Ottley School

This school at Britannia House in the Tything, was founded in 1883. It started with just eleven girls and three staff headed by the headmistress, Miss Ottley (1840–1912). Between 1883 and 1914, the school was named 'The Worcester High School for Girls,' before it was renamed 'The Alice Ottley School.' Edward Elgar, a visiting teacher of the violin, was a great friend of Miss Ottley.

After 25 years of teaching, at her school, Alice Ottley retired; she became ill shortly after and died in 1912. On the day of her funeral in Worcester, all the shops closed and blinds drawn as a mark of respect. She was buried in Astwood Cemetery. In 1957, a commemoration window was placed in the Cloisters of Worcester Cathedral.

When the former boys' Royal Grammar School in the Tything, merged with The Alice Ottley School in September, 2007, the name was changed to RGS & The Alice Ottley School. The name was changed yet again in September, 2009, to RGS Worcester.

## All Saints, Deansway

The present church is believed to be at least the third building on this site, it may have started out as a wooden church in Saxon times. A previous All Saints church was damaged in the Civil War. It was rebuilt again in 1715. It is now a Georgian rebuilding of 1742–45, the builders were Richard Squire (Master Mason) and his brother-in-law Richard Davies (Master Carpenter). There was further restoration in 1869; and 1966.

*Left: All Saints Church from 'A Survey of Worcester', Valentine Green, 1764. Right: All Saints Church today*

From 1975, for 20 years, the tower was missing its parapet, because unsafe masonry had to be removed. As a result of a major Tower Restoration Appeal, a completely new parapet was added in 1995

Among its features of interest are the effigy of Edward Hurdman the first Mayor of Worcester 1621, and his wife; the west window stained glass and the four roundels at the end of each aisle, contain fragments of remarkable mediaeval glass and the lower panels in the west window contain beautiful 15th Century glass which may once have been part of the mediaeval east window. The upper panels are fragments of 15th and 17th Century glass. The roundel windows from the north-west corner going clockwise, represent the four authors of the gospels, Matthew, Mark, Luke and John.

## Apollo Cinema

This cinema on Park Street was originally a Zion chapel. It was converted into a cinema in 1911 and was run by three generations of the same family. Entry was 2d for adults, 1d for children – or two empty jam jars for those children who had no money. This cinema closed in 1931 and the building, called Chapel Court, is now converted into flats.

## Arboretum

In the 1700s Barbourne was a hamlet outside the city of Worcester. All the land between Foregate Street, Rainbow Hill and Merriman's Hill, now known as the Arboretum, was a part of a rural open expanse known as Sansome Fields. It was here that a leader of Worcester society, Sir Charles Trubshaw Withers, and his heiress wife chose to build a large villa and lay out Sansome Fields as a park extending to the summit of Rainbow Hill. This popular park, where the people of Worcester could promenade, featured avenues of elm trees, and even a mock Grecian temple. The envy of many towns and cities.

With the death of Withers in the early 1800s, the estate was sold off in lots threatening the continuing existence of this fine public open space. Rescue came in the form of a private group called Worcester Public Pleasure Grounds Company when it bought 25 acres of the land to keep as a public space. The new Arboretum Pleasure Gardens was deigned and laid out by the eminent landscape gardener William Barrow. He created new promenades, terraces, flower and shrub beds, a central fountain, sports facilities and a crystal pavilion. The city council contributed £1,000 towards the cost.

Arboretum Pleasure Gardens opened in 1859, citizens having the privilege of free admission on day a week. The Gardens became an important venue for major public attractions, including: tight-rope spectaculars, concerts and firework displays.

Unfortunately Worcester Public Pleasure Grounds Company went into liquidation in 1866, It must have been a great loss to the people of Worcester, when these pleasure gardens were bought for £13,000 by Worcester Engine Company, a railway locomotive construction firm at Shrub Hill, mainly for the building of workers' houses. The whole park was dismantled and sold; the railings can still be seen at the old Worcester Royal Infirmary, now part of the University.

## Arcade Cinema

The Arcade Cinema once stood in Saint Swithin's Street, between Lettice the draper and Noake Bros. shoe shop. The building was designed in a French renaissance style by Derby-based architectural firm Naylor & Sale.

It opened on 15 March 1913, billed in the Worcestershire Chronicle as 'Worcester's Luxurious Picture House' showing the film 'The Paper Trail'. It was soon taken over by the Provincial Cinematograph Theatres chain. and that in turn in 1929 was taken over by the Gaumont British Theatres chain.

The Arcade Cinema was closed in November 1935. The Gaumont Cinema opened shortly afterwards in Foregate Street as a replacement. Today the site has no evidence of the cinema and is part the Superdrug store.

## Astwood Cemetery, Astwood Road

This cemetery was created in 1858, when the churchyard burial grounds were bursting at the seams. William Laslett donated some 20 acres.

Here are just some of those buried here:

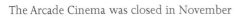

*First person to be buried here was a six-week-old baby, John Ryan in 1858.*

*Sir Charles Hastings (1796–1866), founder member of the BMA (British Medical Association).*

*Alice Ottley, headmistress of Alice Ottley School, who died in 1912.*

## The Athenaeum

The Athenaeum, behind the Museum of Natural History in Foregate Street, was a gift from William Laslett, and was erected in 1834.

Inside the building was a lecture hall, also used as an exhibition space where John Constable (1776–1837) exhibited some of his paintings. There was also a reading room, a library, and even a laboratory.

The Athenaenum also held evening classes in music and French, as well as mathematics. with the subscription at three shillings per quarter.

## Austin House, Castle Street

County Furnishings has occupied Austin House since 1990. Designed by noted Scottish architect John Carrick Stuart Soutar and completed around 1939, this functional brick building incorporated a garage, car repair shop and car showroom. The design is lifted by a tapering sided square tower topped by an open lantern, this clock tower is a distinctive landmark in the city. Since its completion just before World War II, the building remained a site for the sale and repair of motor vehicles. Initially it was occupied by H A Saunders Limited, and later by Mann Egerton, before County Furnishings converted into its furnishing store.

H A Saunders was a national chain of motor car agents based on Finchley Road, London. The Worcester branch of H A Saunders was built on part of the site of the County Gaol which had been designed by Francis Sandys and built 1809–1813, but demolished in the later 19th century. Its castellated appearance led to the naming of the street.

The importance of the design of Austin House was recognised at last, and it was given a Grade II listing in 2012.

## Berkeley's Hospital, Foregate

This Hospital, an important example of Renaissance planning and one of the finest almshouse groups in England, is a stone's throw away from Foregate Street railway station. It was founded in 1692, by a bequest of £2,000 in Robert Berkeley's will, to house 'twelve poor men and just one woman'.

Robert Berkeley (1584–1656) born in Worcester, the son of Rowland Berkeley and Catherine Hayward, who was the daughter of Thomas Hayward, was an English judge and politician. He sat in the House of Commons from 1621 to 1624, and in 1611 he inherited Spetchley on the death of his father.

The almshouses, each with a shield of the founder's Arms over its doorway, face each other in two rows. In front of Berkeley Hospital is a beautiful well-kept lawn. At the opposite end to the gateway, is a beautiful chapel, dated 1703. It forms a delightful centrepiece, with its statue of the founder placed above its door.

## Bone Mill

This Grade II-listed Bone Mill, with its two floors of grinding pans, was one of only two surviving steam driven mills, and the only surviving porcelain grinding mill in

England. It was designed by Robert Armstrong in 1851–52. The current Berkeley Group has sensitively refurbished this area, historically home to the Royal Worcester Porcelain Company. It has created a commercial venture called 'The Waterside', which is an eight acre commercial, living and leisure development. There were very strong objections from several heritage and other conservative groups at the planning stage of The Waterside development.

## Britannia Square

Britannia Square has some of the most impressive town houses, which were built around 1820. Young Edward Elgar used to call on No 11 for his piano lessons.

## Britannia House

Britannia House, a Grade II-listed house in the Upper Tything built between 1730 and 1750, supposedly designed by Thomas White, a local stone carver who was also credited as the sculptor during the building of the Guildhall years earlier. In the centre of the facade sits the majestic figure of Britannia the goddess of the Romans, who has become a figure of national personification of the United Kingdom. It became Alice Ottley School in 1883 and continues as RGS.

## Cinderella Shoe Works

The Cinderella Shoe Works factory building in Watery Lane, Saint Johns, has been developed and reworked into 30 loft-style apartments by Barratt Homes, with a further 70 homes built on the surrounding land; the development is named Willis Place after the founder of Cinderella Shoes.

With the decline of Worcester's glove industry at the beginning of the nineteenth century, boot and shoe factories were set up to make use of the population's leather-working skills, the most famous being Cinderella Shoes, founded by Henry Willis in 1848. It was one of the largest and was one of the first in Worcester to make clever use of a brand name as a marketing tool. The firm sold to customers all over Britain and even sold in the British colonies through the use of travelling salesmen.

Henry was joined in business by his brother James in 1860, they went on to build a purpose built factory in College Street. At the beginning of the 20th century, James took over after Henry's death, at that time he was employing more than 350 people.

In 1914 the firm moved to Watery Lane into a purpose-built factory, with J.F. Willis Ltd. lettering over the main entrance on the front facade. But then the company fortunes changed. Changes in fashion and foreign competition had a direct impact on local companies, and demand for Cinderella Shoes and their products decreased.

The firm was taken over several times before the shoe works closed for good in 1976.

## City Museum and Art Gallery

Worcester Museum was founded in 1833 by members of the Worcestershire Natural History Society, and set up temporarily in rooms on Angel Street. It is claimed to be one of the oldest regional museums in the country. In 1835 a new building where the present-day Odeon now stands on Foregate Street, was built to house the growing collections.

This was named the Hastings Museum after Sir Charles Hastings, president of the Worcestershire Medical Society and a consultant physician at Worcester Infirmary. He is also famous for helping to set up the British Medical Association.

Unfortunately, during the 1860s the museum fell into a decline and the artefacts in the museum were neglected. To the rescue was the Free Libraries Act 1879, being adopted in Worcester. In 1884, a campaign started in the city to build a combined museum, library and school of art and science in time for the jubilee of Queen Victoria, thereby giving it the name of Victoria Institute. The Museum, Art Gallery and Library were amalgamated and given renewed funding.

In 1894 The Duke of York, the future King George V laid a foundation stone for a new building to house the Museum, Art Gallery and Library. The City Museum and Art Gallery 1896 designed by J.W.Simpson and Milner Allen is an outstanding example of late 19th century municipal architecture of this type. Architectural historian Sir Nikolaus Pevsner called it 'a resourceful and animated, totally asymmetrical composition in a mixed Tudor and Baroque style.'

This building was opened to the public in 1896 and became the home of Worcester City Art Gallery, Museum and Library, as well as the School of Art and Science on the Sansome Walk side. This fine building in Foregate Street offers a variety of art exhibitions, events, and workshops, in the Spirit of Enterprise Gallery. There is also a museum which portrays, amongst other gems of history, the history of the Worcestershire Regiment and the Worcestershire Yeomanry Cavalry.

The library moved out of this building in July 2012, relocating to The Hive, a vision 10 years in the making, created with the collaboration of two key partners: the University of Worcester and Worcestershire County Council.

## Cardinal's Hat Inn, Friar Street

The earliest reference to the Cardinal's Hat was in 1497, the inn was designated as one of the depots for the City's fire hooks, which were implements used to pull down burning parts of buildings to prevent the spread of fire. In 1518, Nicholas Mocock was running The Cardinal's Hat Inn. Documents dated 1748 state that the new name was to be 'Swan and Falcon', to address the unpopularity of Roman Catholicism. In 1814, to gain popularity with the Earl of Coventry, the inn was named 'Coventry Arms'. The original name of the inn.'The Cardinal's Hat,' was restored in the 1950s. It is considered one of the oldest pubs in Worcester.

## Commandery, Civil War Centre, Sidbury

The Commandery, a Grade I listed site, after its £1.5 million revamp is definitely worth a visit. It was formerly called the Hospital of Saint Wulstan, and was built in 1085, by Saint Wulstan, Bishop of Worcester (the last Saxon bishop in England), a few years before his death in 1095.

The Commandery became royalist headquarters during the civil war of 1651. The Fort Royal Park was originally in the grounds of the Commandery.

The Commandery covers six periods of history:

### The Monastic Period

*From 1285 to 1480, it was a hospital, where for almost 200 years it cared for sick, as well as offering accommodation to weary pilgrims.*

*Later it began to receive money in return for the care and accommodation, very quickly becoming a retirement home for the well-off.*

### The Tudor period

*During the dissolution, the hospital was seized by Henry VIII, who, in 1540, granted it to Richard Morysyne on payment of £14 3s 5d. A clothier, Thomas Wylde, first rented the Commandery from him for £40 per annum. In 1545 the building was sold to Thomas Wylde, who turned into a family home. His son, Robert Wylde became a very wealthy and successful cloth trader, when he died he left intimate documents about Tudor life. The house remained in the Wylde's family for over two hundred years.*

### The Civil War Period

*This was the most memorable period in the Commandery's history. In 1651 the house was the headquarters of the Royalist troops. At the height of the battle around Sidbury Gate, many troops on both sides were killed.*

Parliamentary forces stormed the Royalist defences. Cromwell's manoeuvre in crossing the River Severn had weakened the Royalist positions on Red Hill and Perry Wood. Charles II, watching the battle from the tower of Worcester Cathedral, rushed down and personally rallied his troops for an attack on the Parliamentarians east of the river. The Royalist attack was two-pronged: Charles himself commanded the thrust against Red Hill while the Duke of Hamilton attacked Perry Wood. The penultimate stage of the battle was fought in the grounds of the Commandery, where the Royalist commander, the William Hamilton, Duke of Hamilton, sustained wounds from a musket ball that shattered his leg, which proved to be fatal. He was buried in Worcester Cathedral. The Battle of Worcester was the final crushing defeat of the Royalist cause. The English Civil War ended at the place where it had started with Prince Rupert's dashing victory at Powick Bridge nine years earlier, in 1642.

### The Georgian period

Thomas Wylde IV was a Member of Parliament for Worcester (1701 to 1727). Being an MP was expensive in those days, especially if elections were contested. He sold the property to John Dandridge in 1764. Three years later it became the home of two middle-class families who shared the house, the Cameron family (who had one daughter and two sons) and the Dandridges.

'Ye Antient Commandery,' from the Court Yard. from a sketch by Theo. Moore, Esq., Architect, London.

Doctor Thomas Cameron's daughter, Mary, was apparently quite a 'little madam', spending a lot of her time in London. Charles was endeavouring to become a doctor like his father. Then there was Henry, the black sheep, who was later cut off from his family, because of the woman he married.

John Dandridge was married in 1776, to Judith Holcombe. They had three sons and a daughter, named Barbara Marie. When Barbara married Richard Mugg Mence, barrister, in 1805, she became the last survivor of the family. Thus Richard Mugg Mence inherited the Commandery. He made some big changes to the place. He died in 1864. His only daughter, also named Barbara, died before him, so the property passed to his nephew Richard Mence, Vicar of Bockleton, Tenbury.

### The School period

In 1866 the Commandery was leased to the Revd. R.H. Blair, who established a College for the Blind. Although only open for the sons of gentlemen, it was a pioneering institution. It gave these boys an education that was sufficient to get them into university or a professional career. In 1887 the school moved to Powick. Today New College Worcester is one of the leading residential schools and colleges for the blind or partially-sighted in Britain, it can trace its history back to these humble beginnings at the Commandery.

## The Littlebury Period

In 1988 it was the home of Littlebury & Co. Ltd. a family business, incorporating Worcester Press. The Littlebury family leased the Commandery as a printing works and bought the whole premises in 1905. Joseph Littlebury made dramatic improvements to the site and its buildings, eventually opening the Great Hall to the public at selected times of the year.

In 1973, the building was bought by the Worcester City Council, who converted it into a museum. It became a Civil War Centre in 1985.

In 2006 the centre was closed to the public. Then, having undergone a £1.5 million revamp, reopened its doors on May 26, 2007.

A sculpture created in 2010 by Lawrence Walker, a Herefordshire blacksmith, in memory of Stuart McNidder MBE, City Council Architect and Planning Officer

## The Cornmarket

This area of Worcester has been a victim of much development. In the Cornmarket, the Plough Inn was replaced by a Jaguar garage, now a bed store, and soon to be swallowed up by the Saint Martin's Quarter development.

The Public Hall was built in 1849, originally as a corn exchange but it was not a commercial success and was converted into a public hall for more general uses and concert hall, abandoned in favour of a corn exchange in Angel Street. It played host to such people as Charles Dickens, Dvorak, and Edward Elgar. Elgar himself conducted the premières of Froissart and The Black Knight, his first two substantial works composed during the early 1890s in this hall. At the evening performance on 13 September 1905 he conducted the Festival Chorus at 'Three Choirs Festival', the only Festival event not held in the cathedral.

The Public Hall was demolished in 1966 to make way for the City Walls road development and a new car park, and what has been called 'possibly the ugliest car park in the country'.

## Cripplegate Park, New Road

The beginnings of the park were in 1878 when a Public Health Act was passed by the City. The name has nothing to do with cripples; it's an old English word for 'low opening in the fence or wall,' enabling sheep to move from field to field. The park, transformed from a refuse tip, opened in 1922. It was made larger in 1932, and ran opposite Worcester's cricket ground. It was opened by Edward, Prince of Wales, and Stanley Baldwin.

Sons of Rest, which started in Birmingham in 1927, to promote leisure and social activities for men over 60. Introduced a small building in the park which dates from at least 1932 and the Prince's visit. Working alongside the Council are the 'Friends of Cripplegate Park,' who introduced bands, etc.

In the centre of the park is a fountain (right), cast in 1858 by Hardy & Padmore, Iron Founders, Worcester. This Grade II-listed fountain was previously sited in the former Market Hall on Pump Street, introduced in order to give relief from the stifling heat within the hall, it was presented as a gift by Richard Padmore and installed on 21st March 1859. In 1922 the fountain was found to be leaking at a time when the hall was suffering from many structural faults, the repair of the fountain was just not a priority. It was presented to the park that same year and has become a focal point ever since.

**Crowngate Shopping Centre, Friary Walk**

Crowngate Shopping Centre the most prominent shopping area undercover. It was opened in 1992, and is owned and managed by 'The Crown Estate.' Crowngate is supported by two smaller shopping centres: the older Cathedral Plaza (previously called the Lychgate Centre) which was opened in 1968 and Reindeer Court Centre, opened in 1990.

**Crown Passage, Crown Inn, Crown Hotel**

The entrance to the Crown Passage shopping parade is in Broad Street. It was here where the Crown Hotel once stood at numbers 10 and 10A with Crown Passage, and including Crown Inn. If you look up at the entrance, you will see the ornate George IV lamp and Regency ironwork; all part of the frontage of the Crown Hotel. The Crown Hotel was one of the principal coaching inns of Worcester. Several houses in Broad Street are known to have 17th century and earlier origins numbers 32, 40, 41 and 57. Already by the 16th century Broad Street was second only to High Street in commercial importance.

**Diglis Bridge**

The Diglis Bridge, positioned just south of Diglis Island, is Worcester's latest river crossing, which opened in July, 2010. Work started in November, 2009 and was funded partly by Sustrans' Connect2 Project and Worcestershire County Council.

This cycle and pedestrian bridge links the

Navigation Road in Diglis with Lower Wick, thus connecting the cycle and walking paths on both sides of the River Severn, making a complete circuit, providing vital links for Worcester, Malvern and Powick residents. It uses route 46 of the National Cycle Network which significantly enhances links between Saint Johns and Cherry Orchard, Red Hill and Saint Peters.

Sustrans awarded £850,000 towards the project, Worcestershire County Council contributed a further £1.5 million on the construction of the Diglis Bridge and a further £450,000 on the development of connecting walking and cycling links. Worcester City Council contributed an additional £1m which has been spent on developing the riverfront between the New Road Bridge and Diglis Island.

The impressive structure is a painted steel single cable stay bridge. The 'A' frame pylon rises over 28 metres above the west bank and is inclined towards the river at 22.5 degrees. The pylon is anchored by four pairs of solid steel cable back stays, which in turn supports the deck with a further five pairs of solid steel cable stays. The deck, which spans 66 metres across the river, is a minimum of 3.5 metres wide between the top wooden handrails and weighs approximately 70 tonnes.

## Diglis House

This 18th century house on Severn Street, close to Worcester Cathedral, was built in the 1800s during the reign of George III. It is believed to have been built on the site of a previous house belonging to William Berkeley and destroyed during the Civil War in 1643.

It was the home of Edward Leader Williams, the Chief Engineer to the Severn Navigation Commission. His son, Benjamin Leader Williams was born in the house in 1831 and became famous as a landscape artist. He reversed his name to Benjamin Williams Leader, in 1857, to distinguish himself from the many other painters with the surname of Williams. He joined the Royal Academy (London) as a Royal Academician in 1898. His very famous painting 'February Fill Dyke' is on display at the Birmingham Museum and Gallery.

The artist, John Constable, was a frequent visitor to Diglis House. In recent times this house has been beautifully restored to become one of the finest hotels in the Severn Valley. It is a hotel, restaurant, bar and conference centre with an unrivaled position on the banks of the River Severn.

Worcester Civic Society unveiled the first blue plaque in Worcester, remembering Benjamin Leader Williams, on a wall just outside the hotel, on the river walk.

## The Worcester Porcelain Museum
*Dyson Perrins Museum*

The Worcester Porcelain Museum houses the world's largest collection of Worcester Porcelain. The ceramic collections, archives and records of factory production, form the primary resource for the study of Worcester porcelain and its history. It was opened to show the extensive collection of Richard William Binns. As Managing Director, Art Director and first company historian, he started to buy examples of early Worcester and other international works of art to inspire his workforce. Unfortunately the collections of bronzes and porcelain from other countries, over 10,000 objects, were sold by Royal Worcester soon after the death of Binns in 1900.

Charles William Dyson Perrins, a wealthy, local benefactor formed one of the most important private collections of 18th century Worcester Porcelain. He purchased the museum collection and library in 1926, on the understanding that it would remain on display at the factory for his lifetime. In the 1934 he purchased the Royal Worcester factory, formed a new company and became its chairman. During the Second World War the museum collections were packed and hidden in cellars in Worcester and at Madresfield Court, Malvern. In 1946 Dyson Perrins created the Perrins Museum Trust to administer and unite his own private collection of Worcester porcelain with the former factory museum collection. The combined collections of Worcester Porcelain were re-displayed in the former company showrooms and were exhibited to the general public in June 1951. The new museum was opened by HRH Princess Elizabeth when she visited the factory as part of Royal Worcester's Bicentenary celebrations. To ensure the museum had a permanent home, Dyson Perrins' widow, Frieda, provided the capital to re-house the collections in the Saint Peters School buildings next to the factory in 1967. In the late 1990s the museum was totally re-furbished and the display space doubled, thanks to a grant from the National Lottery and the generosity of many charitable trusts, companies and individuals.

The Museum has changed its name from The Dyson Perrins Museum to The Worcester Porcelain Museum in order to make the collection easier to promote.

## Edgar Tower

Edgar Tower, formally known as Saint Mary's Gate, was built in the mid-14th century. It was a fortified gateway and the main entrance to the royal castle and priory. After a devastating fire in 1202 which swept through the city of Worcester destroying many houses and severely damaging the Cathedral, burning down the gatehouse, the

gatehouse was rebuilt from 'wood and stone of the best quality' on King John's orders. The original figural statue may have been the Virgin Mary, which would have been destroyed during the Reformation. The replacement, a statue of King Edgar (crowned by Oswald in 973), is why it was renamed Edgar Tower.

This original statue of that early monarch, sitting crossed legged, looking down on all those who passed through the gate, slowly disintegrated. In 1910, an exact copy was created during restoration work.

*King Elgar Tower, from 'A Survey of Worcester', Valentine Green, 1764*

Edgar Tower was once the entrance to a Roman camp. It was also the entrance to a monastery, but today leads to College Green, the rear of the Cathedral and buildings of the King's School.

## Fort Royal Park

This park overlooking the city, was built by the Royalists in 1651; this sloping green area was once the site of the Duke of Hamilton's Fort, there to defend the city during the 'siege' in 1646,

During the final battle of September 3, 1651, which became a Parliamentary victory, the Essex militia intermingled here with the retreating Royalist army, creating skirmishes in and around the city.

David McCullough, historian, in his biography of John Adams (1735–1826), wrote: 'Adams, when he visited Worcester in 1786, was deeply moved but disappointed at the locals' lack of knowledge of this Worcester's battle.' McCullough is quoted as saying:

*'The people in the neighbourhood appeared so ignorant and careless at Worcester that I was provoked and asked 'And do Englishmen so soon forget the ground where liberty was fought for?*

*Tell your neighbours and your children that this is holy ground, much holier than that on which your churches stand. All England should come in pilgrimage to this hill, once a year.'*

During 2012 Worcester City Council announced plans for a number of improvements to Fort Royal Park. These will include creating a new play area, repairing the wall on Wylds Lane, dealing with the knotweed invasion on the London Road and installing non-coin operated binoculars so that visitors can enjoy the views afforded from the top of this historic hill. Heritage Lottery Funding will help meet the associated costs.

## Fownes Hotel, City Walls Road

This fine building was a Victorian glove factory which was constructed between 1884 and 1887. In 1887 Fownes Gloves moved into Worcester, from Cheapside, London, under the name of John Fownes and Sons (Thomas and Edward); and at that time the factory was employing over 1,000 workers.

It's a lovely reminder of the fact that gloves had been made in this city for over six hundred years; and the companies of both Fownes and Dents were to become the leading glove manufacturers in Europe.

In 1974, there was a decline in the glove industry due to fashion changes. The manufacture of gloves was moved to Warminster, Wiltshire, and the Worcester factory became derelict.

It is said, on this site of Fownes Hotel in City Walls Road, once stood a nationally known mineral spring, which was reputed to possess very special health giving properties. During the 18th century the craze for 'taking the waters,' had its effects on this city, which almost became a spa town.

The building was restored in 1987, to become the 61-bedroom hotel we see today.

## Gaumont Cinema

This cinema in Foregate, now a bingo hall, opened on 28 October 1935, celebrated as at the cutting edge of cinema technology. The Gaumont, designed by W E Trent and Earnest Tulley and built by Provincial Cinematograph Theatres who were a subsidiary of the Gaumont British Theatres chain.

The opening advert boasted the cinema had 1,740 seats, some of which were specially equipped for deaf people and those who were hard of hearing. The advert in the Worcester Evening News for opening night also boasted that the Gaumont offered patrons free parking. There was also entertainment provided by 'John Bee at the mighty illuminated Compton Organ'. The first film shown was 'The 39 Steps' with Robert Donat and Madeleine Carrol.

The Gaumont also had a very large stage: 70 feet wide, 40 feet deep, hence the venue was able to host some of the top rock and pop acts, including:

Buddy Holly played two shows on 11 March 1958, the year before his tragic death in a plane crash.

Cliff Richard and the Drifters (later to be called the Shadows) played here in December 1958, as part of Arthur Howes' 'The Big Teenage Special'.

The Beatles played here twice, once supporting Roy Orbison on his 1963 tour, and once as a headline act, later in the year.

The Rolling Stones also played here twice, in October and December 1963.

Jimi Hendrix played on 2 April 1967, as one of the support acts together with Cat Stevens and Engelbert Humperdinck, on a tour by The Walker Brothers.

David Bowie played one of his last ever gigs, in June 1973, in the guise of Ziggy Stardust.

Mott The Hoople played here on 15 November 1973, at the height of their fame, supported by the then unknown Queen.

The Rank Organisation closed the Gaumont on 4th May 1974 and it was converted into a Top Rank Bingo Club. Today it is a Gala Bingo Club.

## Gheluvelt Park

This park was opened on 17 June 1922, by Field Marshall The Right Honourable Earl of Ypres, to commemorate the heroic actions of the 2nd Battalion Worcestershire Regiment at the WWI Battle of Gheluvelt, which took place outside the city of Ypres in Belgium on 31 October 1914. The 2nd Battalion counter-attacked and the village of Gheluvelt, with its strategic high ground, was recaptured from the German army; over 190 officers and men of the 2nd Battalion were killed or wounded in the battle.

The park has a number of almshouses, built to provide homes for ex-servicemen and still occupied by their families; a foundation stone was laid by Field Marshall Sir William R Robinson, on 15 January 1919. The main entrance has a memorial archway, with a plaque that reads:

*'City of Worcester homes for disabled sailors and soldiers. The houses that form the central block of these homes were erected to commemorate the Battle of Gheluvelt, in which the Worcestershire Regiment took a very distinguished part.'*

**Earlier times:** The Barbourne College, a boarding school for young gentlemen, was opened in the park around 1884, with its gardens and buildings backing onto Lavender Road. By 1909 Barbourne College had closed and was up for sale. In 1918 the land was sold to the Corporation of Worcester. During 1918, plans proceeded with producing a design for the new park, which is first referred to as Gheluvelt Park in December of that year. All the buildings were demolished, to make way for this new park and war memorial houses, which were built in July 1920, to house injured and retired servicemen. In 1922, the whole area was transformed into the glorious park that we see today. A bandstand in the middle of the lake was added in 1923. In 1953 the Sons of Rest pavilion was built, courtesy of the Rotary Club of Worcester.

The Friends of Gheluvelt Park group was formed in 2003, working alongside Worcester City Council, the Duckworth Trust and the Local Residents' Association.

A fun Day took place that year, in the front of the Pump House, raising money for Help For Heroes and the Myeloma Trust. Since then, a variety of events have been held regularly throughout the year.

Five apple trees were planted in Gheluvelt Park in November. 2009 as part of a Greenpeace campaign, to align with an apple orchard that had been planted in the village of Sipson, which was earmarked for total destruction if the proposed third runway at Heathrow was given the go-ahead. Peter Robinson, of Worcester Greenpeace said:

'We are planting these apple trees in the park so that we are twinned with the new apple orchard, which is on the runway site at Heathrow...'

In that same year, on 17 October 2009, a bench was dedicated to the memory of Worcester soldier, Private Jason Williams, of the Second Battalion Mercian Regiment, who was killed in Afghanistan. He was killed by an explosion in Helmand Province in August 2009, while trying to retrieve the body of a fallen comrade.

On 14 August 2010, a revamped Gheluvelt Park, had a Grand Opening. The well-deserved improvements were financed with a £803,000 Heritage Lottery Grant. The park now has a new Splash Pad, a new children's play area, adult exercise equipment and a special World War I interpretative feature (above), made from weathered corten steel panels. This memorial will be used as an open air classroom or schoolchildren to learn the facts and figures of the First World War and the role of the Worcestershire Regiment.

### Glover's Needle

Saint Andrews church with its tall spire, was built by the Saxons. The spire was destroyed in the great storm of 733. In 1757, the spire was rebuilt using an ingenious method of kite flying; carrying the stones up to the building area. In 1949, the church was demolished, leaving just the spire; creating a garden of remembrance.

The people of Worcester were so delighted with this spire, that they named it Glover's Needle in the memory of the local glove-making industry.

## Gregory's Mill

All traces of the mill have long disappeared, the only reminder of Gregory's Mill is the old stone bridge house over the brook, close to the Worcester and Birmingham Canal.

During World War II, the BBC erected radio aerials inside the Gregory Mills brickworks with its tall chimney, which stood on the site of the mill.

## The Greyfriars, Friars Street

The Greyfriars is the finest half-timbered building in Worcester, built in 1480. From the 13th to the 16th century the street was dominated by a Franciscan friary from which Friar Street, and Greyfriars, get their names. Franciscan friars were sometimes called Grey Friars because of their grey habits.

The name of Greyfriars might have come from the house being wrongly associated, from the early twentieth century, with the old Friary, the last building the friars added. In the 1530s Henry VIII dissolved the monasteries and their presence in the street was wiped out.

Built as a town house for Thomas Grene, a wealthy Merchant, influential citizen, and brewer, who had been High Bailiff of Worcester. This timbered-framed building in the City Centre fell into a terrible state of dilapidation during the 19th century. But thankfully, in the 1940s, Mr Matley Moore and his sister Elsie lovingly restored the house, saving it from being demolished. They lived there until their deaths in the 1980s.

Greyfriars is now in the care of the National Trust.

## Guildhall

The Guildhall was built between 1721–3, the current building replaced a mediaeval

timber-framed building. The architect is reputed to be Thomas White; however it is more probably designed by several craftsmen including White, who signed the pedimental sculpture. There were later alterations including those to the Assembly Room interior by George Byfield of 1791 and by Sir George Gilbert Scott and Henry Rowe (municipal architects) in 1878–80. In 1221, the  citizens of Worcester were granted a charter, which among other things allowed them to establish a guild of merchants to take control of the trade in the city. Hence the name. The first Guildhall (known as the Town Hall) was a timber-framed structure. It contained the courts of justice, one at each end of the building. It also contained a prison with its notorious dungeon.

Within the central three bays; framed by two huge Corinthian pillars, is an elaborate war-like trophy, carved and signed by Thomas White. He also carved the statue of Queen Anne which can be seen over the entrance to the Guildhall. Over the main doorway of the Guildhall it reads: 'Floreat Semper Fidelis Civitas' (Semper fidelis: always faithful; floreat: flourish; Civitas: city/citizen).

On the parapet of the Guildhall are five allegorical figures which depict from left to right; Hercules (as Labour), Peace, Justice, Plenty and Chastisement with an axe. Above the doorway there is a stone head which is nailed by its ears; said to be that of Oliver Cromwell. On one side of the entrance is the statue of Charles I, holding a miniature church, while on the other side is Charles II, with orb and sceptre.

Rare Georgian hunting wallpaper hangs in the parlour. In the lower hall there are many portraits of merit, which include:

A portrait of George III by Reynolds.
A portrait of George III and his Queen, given by the King to the Earl of Coventry.
A portrait of Sir Edward Elgar.

*Two of the statues above the tympanum: Peace and Justice*

On either side of the staircase leading up to the first floor are boards which list the Freemen of the City, starting with Lord Nelson in 1702. In the great hall there are fine 16th century tapestries and some 17th century furniture. Hanging on the wall in the ground floor vestibule there is an unusual collection of 48 leather buckets. These were bought in 1729 to fight fires – buckets filled with water were passed through a chain of men.

## The Hive
### Library and History Centre

In 2010 building work began on this £60m 'super library' in The Butts, on the site of the City Council's former vehicle depot. It sits alongside the new University Campus which was developed on the site of the old Royal Infirmary Hospital. The Hive has been ten years in the making and is the result of the vision and commitment of two key partners: the University of Worcester and Worcestershire County Council.

The Queen officially opened the building on 11 July 2012. The 16,000 gold-coloured tiles gleaming in the sunshine after the rain of that morning.

The Hive is 10,000 square metres of public space over five floors, contains a quarter of a million books, has 800 study stations and stores over 26,000 records of historic monuments and buildings. It stands on the banks of the River Severn and uses energy generated by the river to help cool the building.

The project has been funded by £40.9m of Private Financial Initiative (PFI), £6.6m from the county council, £10m from the university, £7m from Advantage West Midlands and £300,000 from Worcester City Council.

## Hop Market Hotel, The Foregate

The Hop Market was established in 1731 in the buildings of the parish workhouse. It was the largest and most profitable in the kingdom, its profits going to the relief of the poor rates. It remained a workhouse until 1794, when a union workhouse was formed in Tallow Hill. The original Hop Market Hotel jutted out to take up more than half of Forest Street, which we know today as The Foregate. In the 1890s Forgate Street had to be widened, to accommodate the rapid growth of city traffic of horse-drawn trams and carriages, and most of the east side was demolished.

The new hopmarket and hotel, built for the Corporation by A.B. Rowe, was flamboyant and decorative, and is now one of the most striking buildings in the city. It was a monument to the prosperity of the city at the turn of the 20th century and to the importance of hops to the commercial life of Worcester.

Walking through its archway into the courtyard, which was once the centre of the hotel, we now find shops and flats. Here also, is a rather delightful café called 'Time to Eat.' It serves home-made food and, in my opinion, serves the best bacon sandwich in Worcester. Jill McCallister and her staff are very friendly; the atmosphere so peaceful as here the café is well away from all the noisy traffic.

## Hop Pole Inn, Foregate Street

The Hop Pole Inn stood on the corner of Foregate Street and Shaw Street; on this site stood the first poor house in Worcester.

The Hop Pole Inn was built when the city was just recovering from the events of 1651, the Battle of Worcester. The Inn was first mentioned in the Saint Nicholas parish records of 1742.

Lord Nelson and Lady Hamilton visited Worcester in 1802, for just a few days. They stayed at the Hop Pole Inn. Queen Victoria stayed here in 1830, when she was visiting Worcester as the Princess Victoria.

During the 18th and 19th century the original Hop Pole Inn was one of the most important inns in Worcester. It was taken over by a Mr Scott in 1842 but shortly after it ceased to be an inn and became a high-class shop called Victoria House. In 1865 it became Scott and Oram.

Twenty years later Richard Westwood took the shop over; later to be followed by W K Hogben of Bond Street, London. In 1926 the building became Fearis's grocery shop.

At the beginning of the 1900s Worcester had the largest hop market in the country and boasted of having seven major breweries, and many pubs brewing their own beer.

## Huntingdon Hall, Crowngate

The 'Countess of Huntingdon Church' was built as a chapel in 1773, by the very formidable Selina, Countess of Huntingdon. She was the founder of the Calvinistic/Methodist group. The last service held here was in 1976.

The chapel, is Grade II-listed. It was about to be demolished in 1990 because it was in need of so much repair, and because it was close to the new construction of the Crowngate enterprise. But a very determined group of people fought hard for ten years to save it, and succeeded by raising £1 million. The building was then restored retaining many original features; some original pews still exist.

There is a rather unique curved staircase leading up to a pulpit, which is flanked by two very splendid eagle lecterns. The communion rail remains beneath the stage.

Huntingdon Hall is a popular concert and entertainment venue, and boasts of outstanding acoustics. When John Betjeman visited Huntingdon Hall, he declared that the hall was: *'unique and irreplaceable... A Georgian gem.'*

## Inns, taverns and alehouses

At the turn of the century Worcester boasted of having around 200 inns, hotels and beer retailers. There were many ancient coaching inns in Worcester, such as the Bell, the Crown, the Star and Garter, and the Unicorn. Alehouses were ordinary dwellings where the householder served homemade ales as well as beer. Inns were purpose-built to accommodate the traveller, and the taverns invariably sold wine and catered for the rich townsfolk. Here are just a few:

The Pheasant, 25 New Street.
The Punch Bowl Inn, College Street, demolished in 1965.
Fountain Inn, Severn Street, demolished in 1935.
Ye Olde Talbot, opposite Worcester Cathedral, originally a 13th century coaching inn.

Saracen's Head, The Tything, originally a house 1800.

The Bear Inn, demolished in 1930s.

Dewdrop Inn, Lower Broadheath, recently restored; few minutes walk from Elgar's birthplace.

Unicorn Hotel, one of the principal coaching inns of Georgian Worcester. Its entrance, is now entrance to the Crowngate Shopping Centre.

The Eagle Vaults, Friar Street since 1859; Young's Mug House in 1779, the Volunteer 1814–17, then as the Plummer's Arms.

The Farriers Arms, Fish Street, originally two houses.

The Lamb and Flag Inn, The Tything.

Mug House Inn, Claines Lane, 1600s.

The Plough Inn, Fish Street, once a house 1850.

The Slug and Lettuce Inn, Queen Street, previously The Sheaf 1659 owned by Robert Fisher; The Rodney 1778; formerly been known as Dingles Coffee House, The Tubs, The King Charles and The Barrels became The Slug and Lettuce in 1984.

## Kay & Co Ltd

Worcester was the home of the famous mail-order company, Kays, although in its heyday the company had many offices and warehouse located in many areas of the U.K.

Kays can trace its heritage back to a jeweller and watchmaker based in Goose Lane, Worcester, now Saint Swithin's Street. The shop was the original home to John Skarratt, an apprenticed clock and watchmaker from London, who founded his business in 1794 in these premises.

*The fine Kays lettering over the doorway of the Foregate building, now the entrance to a sports gym*

His business grew and prospered. By 1814, Skarratt had moved his business to number 2 Broad Street. The shop was expanded sometime in the mid-1860s and was renumbered to number 3 Broad Street.

William Kilbourne Kay moved to Worcester in the early 1870s and took employment with the grandson of the original John Skarratt, John Martin Skarratt, who had taken over the running of his grandfather's and father's business.

In 1886 Kay left the employ of Skarratt and went into partnership with a local architect named George Jones. The two gentlemen started up their own jewellery and watch business, known as Kay, Jones & Co of Worcester, from premises in The Foregate.

By 1890, Kay and Jones dissolved their partnership, but Kay remained in the Foregate premises and changed the name of the company to Kay's of Worcester. He employed four staff, comprising two clerks, an errand boy and himself. The early catalogues were filled with handbills of his product range: jewellery, watches, clocks and household items.

The company had its own premises at number 4 The Foregate between 1886 and 1894, but expanded in 1894 to a site in Shrub Hill Road. These impressive buildings had originally been built for a railway engineering company in the 1850s.

In a twist of fate, Kay entered into discussions during 1896 to buy out John Martin Skarratt, the man who gave him his first job in Worcester. The two businesses were amalgamated in the May of that year. There was a very important aspect to this amalgamation: Skarratt & Co held a contract with the Great Western Railways (GWR) to supply 'clocks, watches and timepieces' and this contract passed to Kay & Co Ltd.

During the twentieth century many of the items featured in the catalogue were manufactured in the factory in Shrub Hill Road, in particular the watches and clocks were assembled, by hand, in Worcester.

During 1906–07 new offices were developed adjacent to Saint Oswald's Hospital in the Tything. Number 23 The Tything was the centre of all of Kays' activities and the company's home for the next 94 years.

By the mid 1920s, William Kilbourne Kay was suffering ill health; and Jack Kilbourne Kay, his youngest son, resigned his commission in the Army to take up a directorship in the company in 1926. William died in May 1929. Four years later Tom Kilbourne Kay, the eldest son and Managing Director, died as a result of contracting pneumonia after sleeping in a damp bed while on business in London. Edwin became Chairman and M.D. with Jack as the joint M.D. However, they decided to sell the business and started to look for a suitable buyers.

In 1937, the majority of the company's shareholdings, held by the Kay family, were sold to Great Universal Stores (GUS) of Manchester. A new building was constructed on some land owned by the company along the road from number 23 The Tything. Unfortunately these offices caught fire in May 1941 and were totally destroyed. The impressive facade was left intact and can still be seen at 9–10 The Tything. New single-storey office accommodation was built behind this impressive frontage after the war finished.

In 1951 Kays expanded once more and bought an impressive red brick factory in Northwick Avenue, Barbourne in order to cope with the post-war growth in mail-order business. This was used as a warehouse throughout the next two decades. Closed in 1971 and then re-opened as an office three years later, after refurbishment, the Barbourne site remained a major part of the Worcester operations until it closed in 2002. It is now a residential building of luxury flats.

Kays became one of the biggest employers in Worcester from 1889 until 2007, at one time employing up to 900 people.

In Worcester, a new single storey warehouse was built at 202 Bransford Road and this land purchase also gave Kays ownership of the historic Cinderella Sports Ground, the original home of Worcestershire County Cricket Club. The pavilion here still has a Kays' clock in its gable end and this was donated to the WCCC by a member in 1896.

Sadly, in 2006, Shop Direct started to demolish the pavilion and although a conservation order has been placed on the building it has been open to the element. Perhaps the greatest change came in the late 1960s when the development and implementation of the computer systems that were to take the company forward in all of its operations, was approved by the board. Initially the computer team was based in the Saint Oswald's' building at 23 The Tything.

In the late 1960s, another office building was purchased, this time from British Railways, adjacent to the railway station at Shrub Hill in Worcester. In yet another twist of fate, the company had returned, after a period of over sixty years, to its roots. The merchandise buying teams together with the publications department were relocated to the appropriately named, Elgar House

In 1994 Kays celebrated its 200th anniversary. In 2003, GUS sold the entire mail-order operation to March UK Ltd, a company formed by the Wealthy identical twins, the Barclay brothers, Sir David Rowat and Sir Frederick Hugh Barclay. These entrepreneurial businessmen had purchased the Littlewoods mail-order catalogue business in 1997 and the process of amalgamating these two famous names in the mail-order industry started.

## King Charles House

*King Charles House in the 1790s*

The black and white building in New Street is all that remains of a large three-storey mediaeval mansion which once graced the corner of the Cornmarket. A huge fire partly destroyed this mansion, and the remaining building has since been divided into a shop and a restaurant, the King Charles Restaurant. It is one of the oldest restaurants in Worcester.

From 1574, the mansion had been the home of the Berkeley family. It was here that Judge William Berkeley was born in 1684. Later the house passed on to Mr Durant who was host to King Charles II in 1651 just before the Battle of Worcester. It was from this house that King Charles made his escape through the back door, while being pursued by some of Cromwell's men.

The basement was the dungeon, known as the bottled dungeon, where Judge William Berkeley kept his prisoners that were awaiting trial. Upstairs, the restaurant's bar, is apparently where King Charles held meetings with his officers. The ground floor is an oak-panelled dining room, with its open fireplaces, lace tablecloths, crystal glasses, all of which is enhanced by candlelight.

### King's School, Worcester

With its earliest roots in monastic tuition in Worcester as far back as the tenth century, the King's School was one of the seven schools established, or re-endowed and renamed, by King Henry VIII in 1541. On 7 December 1541, Henry VIII personally appointed the school's first headmaster, John Pether. It is situated next to Worcester Cathedral. The senior school is on the College Green, which is on a space between the Cathedral and the River Severn. Much of the school's buildings are leased from the cathedral, including College Hall, which was the monastic refectory.

*The King's School's Michael Baker Boathouse was 'launched' on 28 April 2012. The Boathouse is in the form of an upturned boat and it provides 'state of the art' facilities for the storage and maintenance of King's fleet of boats, as well as provide training facilities for rowers, which will be second to none in the country*

The King's School, and Worcester Cathedral maintain a close relationship; the school providing choristers for the cathedral.

### Lasletts Almshouses, Union Street

William Laslett, MP for Worcester in 1852, bought the former City Gaol, previously a Franciscan Friary, on this site in 1867 for £2,250 converting the cells to almshouses to accommodate old married couples. These almshouses were built to replace the gaol building in 1912.

### Lea & Perrins Factory, Midland Road, Worcester

The famous Worcestershire Sauce is still being made in the Lea and Perrins Midland Road factory, just off and backing onto Wyld's Lane. The Sauce was first produced in 1835. The source of the recipe is still a mystery, but early labels declare that it was 'From the recipe of a nobleman of the county.' The story goes: Marcus Lord Sandys, a local nobleman, returned from one of his offices as Governor of Bengal, India with a recipe. He asked John Wheeley Lea and William Perrins, owners of a local chemist shop, to make up a sauce from that recipe.

John and William made up an extra jar of the sauce for their own assessment, but when they tasted the concoction they did not find it to their liking and put it for storage in the cellar. Months later, they tested it again, and found it had matured into a very pleasant taste. Today, Lea & Perrins sauce is allowed to mature for up to three years before it is sold.

Worcestershire sauce was first sold commercially in 1837. There is a plaque at the end of Bank Street, by the entrance to Crowngate Shopping Centre, which commemorates the original site of John Lea and William Perrins' factory, at number 64 Broad Street in 1837. In just a few short years, it was known and coveted in kitchens throughout Europe.

In 1839, John Duncan, a New York entrepreneur, ordered a small quantity of Lea & Perrins Worcestershire Sauce, and in the space of a few short years Duncan was importing large shipments to keep up with demand. Lea & Perrins was the only commercially bottled condiment in the US, and Americans loved it right away. Over 170 years later, Lea & Perrins sauce remains a favourite in households across the US.

In 1844 increased production prompted storage problems and a warehouse on the Quay was rented. A rented warehouse on Bank Street was added later. In 1864 Lea & Perrins' Sauce Company bought and added another warehouse in Bank Street that had become available. It backed onto the shop in Broad Street, allowing an adjoining door to be built. In 1870 the partners started phasing out the rented warehouse premises.

Output of the sauce grew steadily, and the partners decided to cease trading as chemists, sell off their chemist branches, and devote their time and energy to the manufacture and distribution of their world-famous condiment. In the early 1860s John Wheeley Lea and William

Perrins had been joined in partnership by their sons Charles Lea and James Perrins, and later by Francis Barnitt and William Lyndsay Stewart. The new management started planning a purpose-built factory, but nothing was done until after the death of both founders, James Perrins, and the retirement of the remaining son, Charles. The remaining partners were joined by Charles William Dyson Perrins (known as Dyson), the grandson of the founder William Perrins. There was a renewed pursuit of a new factory. They eventually chose a site in Midland Road. The land was bought from Midland Railway Company and the architect William Henman of Birmingham was employed. His design was a building with two storeys and a steel-framed glass roof over a central courtyard.

Production moved to the Midlands Road factory in 1897, and continues there to the present day. Lea & Perrins was granted a Royal Warrant by King Edward VII in 1904. In 1930 Lea & Perrins was merged with HP Sauce Limited.

There was one major interruption in production, at 8pm on 24 August 1964 a serious and spectacular fire broke out in the factory. It was recorded that this fire was caused by the careless disposal of lighted material in the recreation room on the upper floor. The fire lit up the sky for miles around, hundreds of people in Midland Road, gazed up at a blazing inferno at the Lea & Perrins factory which was confined to second floor and roof. Production of the world-famous Worcestershire Sauce was halted for weeks.

In 1988 Lea & Perrins became part of the BSN Groupe who later changed their name to The Danone Group. In 2005 Lea & Perrins and HP Foods become part of H J Heinz & Co. Limited.

## Lich Gate, Worcester

This was a covered gateway, where coffins may have rested before access to the burial grounds to the north of the cathedral during mediaeval times. It was the last remaining cathedral Lich Gate in the country. It was demolished in the mid-60s together with many Georgian facades and the timber-framed buildings of Lich Street to make way for 215,000 square feet of shopping development. It was named The Lychgate Centre and has since been renamed the Cathedral Plaza.

The word 'Lich' or 'Lych' derives from the Old English 'Lyk' meaning 'body' or 'corpse'.

*A timber-framed house in Lich Street*

## Maggs Day Centre

Saint Alban's church is the oldest church in the centre of Worcester, sitting between Deansway and Worcester College of Technology, it is no longer a church but now it is home to the Maggs Day Centre, a Night Assessment Centre (NAC) which opened in 1985.

It was available for three months every winter, providing shelter for homeless people.

This is the story of why it was founded:

*'In 1984 John Maggs a homeless man in his mid-forties was found dead in an old derelict building near the city centre. John Maggs had a particularly difficult life and spent the last ten years of it sleeping on the streets. As a result of his death a group of people from local churches around the city got together and formed an action group to try and raise funds and awareness to help overcome the issues of homelessness.*

*The Bishop of Worcester offered the use of Saint Albans church as a day centre. Twenty years on and the day centre was still growing from strength to strength, providing invaluable service.'*

Its services include:

*Maggs Day Centre:* a direct access Day Centre offering food, shelter, support, washing/shower and laundry facilities

*Activity Centre:* The Centre runs skills training to help people manage their lives better, such as reading, writing, cooking, art, together with the social skills necessary to reintegrate back into society

*Maggs Clothing Project:* providing free clothes, bedding and domestic items to those in need or hardship across the city.

## Nash House, New Street

This four storey, half-timbered Elizabethan house was built in the 17th century. Before Richard Nash bought the house, it was a furniture shop belonging to the Slade family.

When Richard Nash died in 1605, He left this house to his son, John Nash. The building takes its name from Alderman John Nash (1590–1662), who was Mayor of Worcester and Representative of the City in Parliament during the reign of Charles I.

## Northwick Cinema, Ombersley Road

Built and operated by an independent operator, who also operated the Scala Cinema in the town centre. The Northwick Cinema was designed by Charles E. Wilford, John Alexander designed the interiors. The auditorium had seating for 800 in the stalls and 309 in the circle. It opened on 28th November 1938, and the first film shown at this cinema was 'Test Pilot' starring Clark Gable, Myrna Loy and Spencer Tracey.

The cinema closed in 1966 (it was a bingo hall for 16 years). Property developer, Ian Perks, came to the rescue in 1991, converting the building into a night-spot. Twenty years later the Northwick underwent a very dramatic change; an exhibition hall for Grays Interiors.

The Northwick closed as a full-time cinema on 10th September 1966 with Dean Martin in 'The Silencers' and Audie Murphy in 'Arizona Raiders', It re-opened on 30th September 1966 as a bingo club, and ran as this under several owners, the last being Mecca who closed it in 1982. The building stood empty until it re-opened on 6th June 1991 as an entertainment centre, with John Alexander's beautiful interior fully restored. It was used for live shows and also some film use. This venture lasted until 1996 when the building was boarded-up.

In August 2003 plans were put forward to demolish the cinema and build flats on the site, but these were objected to by the Cinema Theatre Association and were turned down by the local council. The building was given Grade II-listed status and converted into an antiques centre in 2006. The interior plasterwork by John Alexander and many of the original details were totally restored. The side splay walls, close to the proscenium opening, are a wonderful example of Art Deco plasterwork. They are Alexander's only surviving work in a complete and unaltered form. The designs are over-life-size mythical figures, three on each side, who are ascending a marvellous example of an Art Deco style staircase, with many swirls, scrolls and curves. There are also many original 1930s light fittings.

## Odeon Cinema

In 1835 a new building was built to house the collections in Foregate Street on the present site of the Odeon Cinema. The museum was called the Hastings Museum. However this moved to a new site in 1896 leaving the building free to be converted into the Empire Music Hall. It later operated as the Empire Theatre until 1912, when it then became the Empire Picture Palace. Alterations were carried out in 1914 and it re-opened as the Silver Cinema which opened in 1915.

The Silver Cinema closed in the 1930s and the site was purchased by Oscar Deutsch (right) in 1935. Oscar Deutsch (1893–1941), a Birmingham-born son of an Hungarian emigrant, who founded this famous chain of cinemas.

Deutsch obtained planning permission for a replacement cinema and demolished the Silver in 1939, along with the buildings either side, to make room for his big new cinema. However, by the time the structure of the new building, designed by Robert Bullivant, was completed, war had broken out and the building was requisitioned by the government. During World War II, the shell of this new building was taken over by the War Department and used as a storage place for munitions and spare aircraft parts.

Work restarted on the Odeon cinema in 1948, and it opened its doors on 2 January 1950; the first film shown was 'The Rocking Horse Winner', directed by Anthony Pelissier and starring John Howard Davies, Valerie Hobson and John Mills.
The Worcester Evening News reported that a crowd of 5,000 or 6,000 people turned up for the official opening.

As a nice link with the past, the chief projectionist at the new Odeon was E P Rouse, who had held the same post at the Silver Cinema; he served for three years in the Royal Navy between the two jobs.

When it opened the cinema had 1,688 seats and a single screen. Since 1974 it has gradually added more and more screens. Today, the Odeon cinema has seven screens, the biggest seating 273 people.

*The Bishop's Palace, from 'A Survey of Worcester', Valentine Green, 1764*

### Old Palace, Deansway

The Old Palace was the official residence of the Bishop of Worcester until 1842. Standing alongside Worcester Cathedral, the original house which stood on the present site dated back to early 11th century, and at least two internal mediaeval walls of this building survive.

The present palace is a single large building, the present form of the building owes most to a rebuilding programme by the architects William and Francis Smith for Bishop Hough, between 1719 and 1723.

The palace has hosted three royal visits: in 1575 Elizabeth I, her Council and Household stayed here for seven days; James II stayed for three nights in 1687; George III and members of the royal family stayed in 1788, while attending the Three Choirs Festival.

The Bishop's Palace was sold to the Dean and Chapter of Worcester Cathedral in 1846 and it remained as the Deanery until 1941. During the Second World War it was let to the Ministry of Works between 1941–50. It later became a Church Club house and Diocesan offices.

The Old Palace has been a centre of hospitality for over 1,000 years. Bishops and Deans have been entertained here for hundreds of years and now the beautiful building is also available for wedding reception hire and is a centre of Christian hospitality boasting a beautiful beamed hall which serves as the main dining area and the atmospheric 'Abbot's Kitchen' where food and drink have been served for hundreds of years.

### Old Rectifying House, North Parade

Old Rectifying Houses refers to the rectifying of spirits, and at the back of this inn was once a distillery. The main part of the distillery was across the river at the bottom of Tybridge Street. The Williams Distillery was owned by John Williams and in the 18th century was one of the most important distilleries in the Midlands – the distillery's gin was unsurpassed in England

Until late in the 19th Century when the Severn was dredged and locks and a weir were constructed at Diglis to manage the tide (the River Severn was once tidal as far as Worcester), the inn on North Parade was affected by flooding and every year the beer casks had to be rescued and placed above flood level, while provisions had to be supplied by boat and taken in by way of the upstairs windows. Sadly this building, which stands very close to the River Severn, is still constantly under threat of flooding.

If you walk along the outside of the Old Rectifying House along North Parade, you will see a number of plaques that show the level of the flooding the inn has endured over the years. So far, the flooding of July 2007 has yet to be commemorated.

### Old Saint Martin's Church, Cornmarket

This Anglican-Catholic church, built from bricks made from local clay, is one of Worcester's ancient parish churches. It was largely rebuilt between 1730 and 1780; the West gallery was built in the 1800s. The Georgian tower of 1772, has six bells. But the ringing of these bells in their unsafe frame would be very dangerous. So, the idea was to establish a new frame of bells below, which would give the tower ten bells.

*Saint Martin's Church, from 'A Survey of Worcester', Valentine Green, 1764*

The ring of the ten new bells was delivered in August 2011, following the successful campaign to raise £150,000 to restore the old bells and install the new bells But these ten bells, cast at Taylor's Bellfoundry in Loughborough, will serve to do more than just ring out on a Sunday – they have been chosen specially to allow the next generation of bell ringers to learn the ancient art.

It is said that an earlier building of this church is one of five possible churches in which an underage Shakespeare married a pregnant Anne Hathaway in 1582. It is a church close to where William would have signed the Bond and got his marriage licence. The register from the time still exists but has pages missing, pages that cover the very period when Shakespeare's marriage would have taken place, have been mysteriously removed.

## Perdiswell Park

Perdiswell Hall was built for the Wakeman family in 1788. Thomas Wakeman was Mayor of Worcester in 1761. It was sold in 1860 and demolished in 1956, after damage by fire.

The Municipal Airport in this park in the 1920s, was the first of its kind in the world. At the outbreak of World War II the Ministry of Defence took over the park and it became RAF Perdiswell, receiving Fairey Battle fighter bomber planes from the Austin Motor Works at Longbridge. In 1941 Perdiswell Park became a training school for Spitfire pilots. During World War II there was also a prisoner of war camp situated here.

## Pitchcroft Racecourse

Worcester Corporation purchased this 100-acre park for the public in 1899. Pitchcroft Park had its first race on 27 June 1718, a venue for National Hunt meetings. Worcester is one of the oldest racecourses in the country, Roodee at Chester being the oldest.

In the 1750s executions on gallows took place on Pitchcroft. In 1824, over 30,000 spectators paid ten shillings, £40 of today's money, to watch the great bare-fisted prize fight for the 'Championship of England,' of over 80 rounds, between Tom Spring (1795–1851), heavyweight champion of England, and Jack Langan, heavyweight champion of Ireland. The fight went on for over 70 rounds, lasting two and a half hours (Tom Spring won the fight) It was such a big event that people climbed trees and the masts of sailing ships moored nearby on the River Severn to watch; two overcrowded spectator wooden stands collapsed, injuring many people.

On both sides of the racecourse the tree-lined avenues border an area busy with dog walkers, joggers, cyclists and many other public activities, including: an annual firework display, charity runs, visiting circuses, fairs, beer festivals and competitive boating events, aside the four resident football pitches. Regularly during the summer months air balloons use Pitchcroft as a take off point, their baskets full of people rising above Worcester to travel as the wind takes them.

In 1924, Prime Minister Stanley Baldwin, who was president of the Three Counties Show, one of the biggest events of the year going back to 1794, decided to stage the Three Counties Show on Pitchcroft. Sadly, on the day of the show, the heavens opened up, the rain fell and there were floods up to eight feet deep.

By the summer of 2011, Pitchcroft had lost over forty trees on the eastern avenue, mainly due to Dieback, a condition where trees die prematurely and quite often rapidly. Often it is difficult to diagnose the cause of this disease. Sometimes a tree partially recovers by growing new shoots from the trunk, but sadly, in most cases these die off.

### Powick's Bridge and Powick Mill

Visible from all directions, this distinctive chimney of Powick Power Station was built to service the world's first combined steam/hydro-electric power station. It opened in 1894 on the River Teme at Powick; it had four water turbines and three steam engines; supplying half the city of Worcester's needs. Additional power coming on line in 1902 from

the Worcester Power Station on Hylton Road.

This chimney was formerly just a water mill; later to be converted into a laundry, and later still it was turned into residential apartments.

The bridge over the River Teme at Powick, constructed in mediaeval times, was the site of the first 'skirmish' of the Civil War: The Battle of Powick Bridge, fought on 23 September 1642, was the first major cavalry engagement of the English Civil War, a defeat of Robert Devereux, 3rd Earl of Essex, by Prince Rupert. It was also the start of the final battle of the Civil War on the 3 September 1651. The Royalists broke the bridge, but Major-General Richard Deane forced his way over the River Teme and pursued them into Worcester.

### Pump House

The Pump House, by the River Severn in Gheluvelt Park, was transformed by The Duckworth Trust which turned this building into a community environment centre. It was originally two separate buildings. The West Wing was built in 1858,

providing an engine and boiler room. Ten years
later the East Wing was built. Finally in 1902,
the Central Wing was built over a clean storage
tank between the two wings.

A new engine room was added in 1912;
steam pumps partially replaced by electrically
driven ones. In 1998, settlement tanks were
removed. Objectives of the Pump House
Environment Centre were:

1. To provide visitors with the usual facilities plus a public information centre,
   to emphasise sustainability issues, focussing particularly on waste minimisation,
   recycling energy efficiency and water conservation.
2. Provide support and training for environmental volunteers, disadvantaged
   and local groups.
3. Raise environmental awareness among the residents, and in the Worcester schools
   within a wide community.
4. To share and combine the resources of three environmental organisations via
   the establishment of a joint operational base and workshops.
5. To preserve, enhance and give new life to an excellent example of 18th century
   architecture.
6. To demonstrate that you can refurbish old buildings using a wide range of 'green'
   building materials and renewable energy technologies.

This Pump House Environment Centre project was first publicised in June, 2000.
Since then the Duckworth Worcestershire Trust, in association with
a number of parties, obtained planning permission for change of use and the
installation of solar panels, wind turbines and a geothermal heating system.

The Duckworth Worcestershire Trust is a registered charity which was established
in 1998, by former chairman of Worcester Heat Systems, Cecil Duckworth OBE.

The city councillors granted Cecil Duckworth honorary freeman of the city status in
recognition of his city work, sporting investment and business success.

The Friends of Gheluvelt Park group, established in 2003, meets at the Pump House.
It now has over 150 members and was set up so as to provide volunteers, helping to
run the Environment Centre, undertake practical improvement projects within the park
and support the numerous fund-raising events in the park.

The Barbourne Water Tower, alongside the River Severn, was sited opposite
where the Pump House is today and was built as part of the water works in 1770.
The foundations can still be seen today. Water was pumped into the tower through
wooden pipes and then out to the central city supply near the Trinity. The system
became redundant when the new waterworks was built in the 1800s. The Tower
was demolished in the 1960s.

## Queen Elizabeth House

Queen Elizabeth House is a 15th century timber-framed building on Trinity Street. In 1891 the house was jacked up and moved to save it from a road improvement scheme. Mayor Smith-Carrington raised the funds to move this historic building those few yards to its present position.

Queen Elizabeth I is likely to be connected to the building through an endowment to Trinity Hospital, school and almshouses. It has been suggested that this was the schoolmaster's house. The present Queen Elizabeth Almshouses are in Upper Tything.

A complete renovation was carried out in 1995. It is now used by Worcester City Museum.

## Rigidal Systems, Blackpole

Rigidal is one of the world's leading manufacturers of metal cladding for walls and roofs. It provided the roof for the new Wembley Stadium; it also produced roofs for Real Madrid's Santiago Bernabeau ground, the iconic Hong Kong Exhibition Centre, and airports including Heathrow, Dubai and Kuwait.

## Royal Grammar School

The Royal Grammar School, now RGS Worcester, was founded by Bishop Bosel, around 685AD, as a secular monastic school in Worcester, making it one of the oldest in England. The independent RGS was founded before 1291.

Henry VIII founded a new school in 1541, called the Kings School Worcester, based on the former site of the Royal Grammar School. Kings School, Worcester, was given a Royal Charter by Queen Elizabeth I in 1561. It then established a governing body known as the Six Masters, a system that still exists to this day.

Throughout its history, land and buildings have been bought for the school, many of the current buildings were paid for Charles William Dyson Perrins, who was an Old Boy and one of the Six Masters – a member of the school's governing body. Perrins Hall was named after his father James Dyson Perrins, owner of Lea and Perrins Worcestershire Sauce, who went to the school.

A second Royal Charter was granted in 1843 by Queen Victoria, and the title of 'Royal' was bestowed to it in 1869.

The RGS school is a day-school, but up until 1992 it accepted boarders. The boarders resided in Whiteladies house, a building that is rumoured to contain hidden treasure from Charles I which he stashed away when he sought refuge there during the Civil War.

## Royal Worcester Porcelain Works

Before the 18th century porcelain was only made in the Far East. For hundreds of years British potters tried to unlock the secrets of porcelain production and develop a successful formula. Doctor John Wall, a physician, and an apothecary, William Davis began experimenting with materials and processes with this very aim. They soon discovered a method of making a porcelain-type material, and realising that their discovery was one of great importance, they quickly secured the financial backing of 13 prominent local business men in Worcester and opened a factory in Worcester in 1751.

A plate from a service made for Lord Valentia, early 19th century

The first Worcester Pottery Factory, Warmstry House, was situated on the banks of the River Severn and it was from here that after buying out Benjamin Lund's Bristol porcelain factory, in 1752, production went from strength to strength. Wall and Davis had acquired Lund's successful recipes and production techniques needed to move their company forward. The most important of these was how to make soapstone porcelain, or soap rock porcelain. By purchasing special licences to mine soapstone in Cornwall, the Worcester Pottery company went on to produce a new type of porcelain that could hold boiling water without cracking. The huge rise in tea consumption in the 1760s created a massive demand for tea wares, and the Worcester factory prospered during these times.

In the early years virtually everything produced was functional, and by 1755 the Worcester factory was making the best English blue and white porcelain tea wares that

money could buy. It would also start making expensive coloured enamel sets and richly decorated designs for wealthy customers. These wares took influence from and copied porcelain from the Japan, France and Germany.

In 1774 John Wall retired, William Davis took control and the Worcester factory started to concentrate on production of tableware for individual wealthy customers.

In 1783 the Warmstry House factory was purchased by its London agent, Thomas Flight for his two sons Joseph and John. Over the next few years the Flights struggled with countless technical problems, and the departure of their head of the decorating department Robert Chamberlain to form his own company. But their fortunes began to change when John Flight travelled in France to study the latest French porcelain designs and introduced new spiral fluted shapes and French sprig patterns which heralded a period of great success.

In 1788 a royal visit from King George III and Queen Charlotte was to alter the fate of Worcester pottery forever. They toured the factory and ordered a breakfast service in the Blue Lily design. After advice from the King, John Flight opened a prestigious Worcester pottery shop at 1 Coventry Street, London and the following year, in 1789, was awarded the first Royal Warrant, allowing them to use the Royal Coat of Arms and the words 'Manufacturers to their Majestie'.

Through the years the Worcester pottery and porcelain company has changed hands and changed names many times, from Flight to Flight & Barr to Barr, Flight & Barr. Then in 1840 the Flight, Barr & Barr factory joined forces with its former rival, Chamberlain, thus forming Chamberlain & Co., between them evolving new products and ideas to establish the Worcester Company in the Victorian Era. Porcelain continued to be made in Chamberlain's factory in Severn Street, Diglis, where the main factory was to operate thereafter.

In 1851 it was owned and managed by Kerr & Binns who turned the business around and in July 1862 changed the name to The Worcester Royal Porcelain Company taking royal Worcester pottery to new and greater fortunes.

New products were so successful that in 1873, the factory struggled to meet orders, the company had to find a way to expand. In 1874 George B. Ford of Burslem was chosen as the architect for the new factory development and extensive alterations were planned. The main idea appears to have been to organise the factory buildings in a fan shape with the products moving through the various departments from left to right, aiming to reduce the distance the porcelain was moved between processes. For first time it was also proposed to erect significant buildings on a large area of land to the south of the road, bordering the canal. Binns claimed that between 1852 and 1880 the factory had expanded from 80 employees to over 800.

In the 1890s Royal Worcester's fortunes began to turn downwards again. More affordable ranges of decorative wares carried the company through those difficult years, but the factory had to downsize. The twentieth century saw technical changes and expansion in the 1960s and 70s.

In 2005 a large part of the Royal Worcester Severn Street factory site was sold to developers. In 2006 there was major rationalisation and all production, except hand-painted fruit, was now overseas. On 6 November 2008 Royal Worcester and Spode was taken into administration and in 2009 Royal Worcester's name was purchased by Portmeirion Pottery, Stoke on Trent. On the 14 June that same year the Severn Street factory site and shops finally closed.

The Waterside development has refurbished the old factory buildings for flats, created new-build housing and commercial space, giving the whole site a new lease of life.

## Russell & Dorrell

Russell and Dorrell, furniture store, first opened in the High Street of Worcester, in 1834. Mr Russell had bought the business from Thomas Wilks, a tailor.

In 1846 it became Russell and Dorrell after Mr Dorrell's great, great uncle James became a partner, eventually buying out Mr Russell in 1870.

Over the years the business flourished and became a well-known name in the part of the High Street which currently houses Monsoon and Next.

The store moved to County Mills, Riverside, Worcester, in 2003. Sadly it closed down in June 2011 and the building was bought by Worcester College of Technology in 2012.

## Sabrina Bridge

A cable-stayed footbridge built in 1992 for £617,000. As with the much newer Diglis Bridge, it has a single A-frame tower on the west river bank, and has an asymmetric span arrangement. The main span is 62 metres, with a 3 metre-wide deck.

The bridge is generally in steel, with timber deck planks with added anti-slip surfacing.

The plaques, either end, read:

*The span of the bridge is 62 metres, the width is 3 metres and the 'A' frame is 20 metres high. The height from the mean water level is 7 metres and the total weight is 120 tonnes.*

*Designer: YRM Anthony Hunt Associates.*

*Construction: Morrison Shand Construction Ltd.*

## Saint Albans, Deansway

This church has retained nearly all of its mediaeval fabrics. Parishioners were too poor to be able to afford any replacements. A plaque on the wall of Saint Albans reads:

*'Saint Alban's Church may have originated in Roman times, although there is no conclusive evidence to support such an early date. However, it is believed that a church was in existence here by about 720AD.*

*The present building is at least early Norman (about 1175) with possibly some of the stonework being Anglo-Saxon. In common with other surviving mediaeval churches in Worcester, it was heavily restored and altered in the 19th and 20th centuries.*

*The man to become Saint Alban (the first British Martyr) was serving as a soldier in the Roman army during the 3rd and 4th century. He was converted to Christianity by a fugitive priest to whom he gave shelter. They exchanged identities so that he was martyred in the priest's place. His tomb was revered and later the site became a church, then an abbey around which developed the town of Saint Albans (formerly the Romano-British settlement Verulamium). His feast day is celebrated on 22 June.'*

## Saint Helen's Church, Fish Street

Saint Helen's (named after Helen, the mother of Constantine the Great) dates back to 680AD. It is the most ancient church of the City of Worcester, and is said to be on the site of a Roman temple.

Saint Helen's was proclaimed the 'mother church' not only of the Worcester churches, but also of a great number of parish churches, within ten miles of the city.

In the early Middle Ages, many churches had only the status of chapels. There was a 13th century church on this site, but it was destroyed by fire.

Edward Elgar at the age of fourteen often rang the curfew bell which was rung nightly up until 1939, deputising for an old bell-ringer named Sanders, who suffered severely from rheumatism. The church's archive keeps many special documents including the marriage bond between William Shakespeare and Anne Hathaway.

*Saint Helen's Church, from 'A Survey of Worcester', Valentine Green, 1764*

## Saint John's Cinema

Saint John's was Worcester's oldest surviving original cinema building. Opened by the Goodsall brothers on the site of the Old King's Head Inn in July 1914, it was hailed at the time as a technological marvel. In the very early days travellers would go the rounds of cinemas 'selling' the new films. In those days too, there was always a piano, and at Saint John's Ray Haines played, sometimes accompanied by a small orchestra of two violins and a cello.

In 1929 it was the first cinema in Worcester to install sound equipment and showed the city's first 'talkie'. It was 'The Singing Fool' starring Al Jolson, and the crowds were so great that they stretched down to the Bull Ring for the evening performances.

After a fire in 1939, the Cinema was taken over by the Odeon group, and finally closed in 1959, falling a victim of the television. For a time it operated as a nightclub called ZigZags.

At 5am on 17 April 2004, fire crews were called to the a blaze at Saint John's Cinema, just off the Bull Ring, in the fear that trespassers were trapped inside. Years later, the building still stands empty and derelict, in a decidedly sorry state. The site is now awaiting development.

## Saint Nicholas Church, Foregate

God is no longer worshipped at this Grade II-listed church, built in 1730, and confusingly attributed to two possible architects: Thomas White or Humphrey Hollin. This church, which stands on the corner of The Cross and Saint Nicholas Street, is now part of a restaurant chain.

Saint Nicholas Church has been well preserved, it has a very beautiful tower, unlike the traditional square towers of many churches. This church was built to replace a 12th century church that once stood on this site. The area, in mediaeval times, was dominated by a cross, and was the traditional commercial centre of the city.

*Saint Nicholas Church, from 'A Survey of Worcester', Valentine Green, 1764*

Alderman Benjamin Baker took it upon himself, in 1761, to hollow out a vault inside the tower of Saint Nicholas Church, for the body of his sister-in-law. there was a public outcry that was quelled when Alderman Baker gave the parish £20, about £3,000 in today's money.

Aside Mrs Mitchell and a large clock, the tower also has a peel of six bells that haven't been rung since the 1930s, due to an attack of death watch beetle in the timbers supporting them. During a restoration in 1948 a solution was found, that enabled the bells to be sounded again – hammers were installed, operated by ropes on a frame in the belfry, a method known as an Ellacombe Apparatus.

Records show that Saint Nicholas church established the first Sunday school in the city in 1785.

## Saint Oswald's Hospital, Upper Tything

Saint Oswald's Hospital, built in 1873, was founded before the end of the 10th century.

This Grade II-listed building, with its red brick and stone dressings, is probably the oldest surviving complex of almshouses in the country.

An effigy of Saint Oswald stands in the entrance. Saint Oswald, was the Archbishop of York, of Danish ancestry, brought up by his uncle Oda, and sent to the abbey of Fleury in France to become a monk. On his return to England Oswald was consecrated Bishop of Worcester in 961. He died in 992AD.

## Saint Richard's Hospice

Saint Richard's Hospice cares for patients and families in Worcestershire who are living with cancer and other life-threatening illnesses. Each year it gives free care and support to over 2,000 patients and their family member, helping them towards the best quality of life possible.

It is a local independent Worcestershire charity taking its name from Richard de la Wych who was born in Droitwich in 1197 and declared a saint in 1262.

It started in 1984 from the home of Droitwich GP Doctor Jenny Bulman, Honorary Medical Officer before moving to Castle Street in Worcester one year later. Originally founded as Saint Richard's Hospice at Home, in 1985 it merged with the Good Shepherd Hospice Group from Malvern when the name changed to the Saint Richard's Hospice Foundation.

*Saint Richard's Hospice uses the snowdrop as its logo, from a quotation which is a Consolation by Bishop Keble (1792–1886):*

*'I am come to calm your fears; I am come to console you in the absence of bright days, and to reassure you of their return.'*

## Saint Stephen's Church, Barbourne

Saint Stephen's Church was completed in 1862, on land that belonged to Miss Jane Lavender and her sister, Mrs Gutch. The sisters lived at Barbourne House, which was on the north side of Gheluvelt Park. Three glass lights in the main East window of Saint Stephen's are to their memory; Jane Lavender died while this church was being built.

When the Reverend C. Hopton came to Saint Stephen's in 1898, he introduced some alterations which included a new oak front to the organ and a new entrance into the vestry. He left nine years later to become a Canon and then Archdeacon of the Diocese of Birmingham.

Electricity arrived in 1912, and a new vestry was built two years later. Construction of the Lady Chapel was set up as part of Jubilee celebrations in 1912.

In 1916, the Archdeacon of Worcester dedicated the new chapel to the glory of God and in honour of the Blessed Virgin and Saint Wulstan. The church windows are dedicated to the memory of members of the Stallred family who lost their lives in World War I.

## Saint Swithun's Church, Church Street

The earliest reference to this church is when Eudo, Dean of Worcester, gave permission for the nearby Benedictine priory to build a church on his land in 1126. The church was then dedicated to Saint Swithun (Saint Swithin).

Rebuilt in 1734–1736, except for its fifteenth century Tudor tower, the architects were Thomas and Edward Woodward, stonemasons from Chipping Campden, who used stone from their local quarries. In the middle of the nineteenth century the east window was redesigned by Henry Eginton to accommodate new stained glass.

*Saint Swithun's Church, from 'A Survey of Worcester', Valentine Green, 1764*

Saint Swithun's is, both inside and out, a stylish and almost unaltered example of early Georgian church architecture, with few equals in the country. It is almost complete with original furnishings including box pews, font, west-end gallery and altar. A beautiful 'three-decker' pulpit with its carved pelican, is approached by a winding stair, and dominates the centre of this church. A dove above the pulpit represents the Holy Spirit, and alongside is the mayor's pew and ceremonial sword rest.

The fine mahogany-cased organ in the west end gallery of Saint Swithun's is the most complete remaining example from the Gray brothers' workshop in London, it dates from 1795. Very few church organs from the 18th century remain in existence, making the Saint Swithun's example extremely important.

The church was declared redundant in 1977 and was taken under the wing of the The Churches Conservation Trust. A group has been formed, known as the Friends of Saint Swithun's, to help in the upkeep of the building and to encourage its use by the local community.

I visited this simple, yet very beautiful church in August, 2007. There I met Eileen, a charming and knowledgeable church volunteer. Eileen related to me the following information:

*'The present church is built on the site of a 13th century church. We think it was rebuilt between 1734–35, because the wealthy congregation wanted it to be more fashionable and up-to-date.*

*All the pews are numbered. Tablets on the wall refer to merchants, such as drapers and grocers.*

*Nearby, in the Shambles, there were butchers shops, and live cattle, which would arrive and be slaughtered behind the shops. There were open drainage channels in the street to allow fluids and blood to be sluiced away.*

*There is no congregation here now. The building is in the care of the Churches Conservation Trust. There are occasional services held here, but not a regular service.*

*We recently just had a festival and we had over 200 people attend on Saint Swithun's Day. We have Friends of the Church here now, and we have Ray who is the custodian. I feel that the beauty of this church is in its simplicity.'*

The Friends' hard work ensured the chimes of Saint Swithun's church clock would ring out once again, and on 8 July 2007 they did for the first time since 1972.

According to legend, Saint Swithun, bishop of Winchester Cathedral, had asked for a humble grave outside the Cathedral, so that it would be exposed to rain, as well as the feet of his followers. However, during the 10th century, Saint Swithun's remains were moved to a shrine inside Winchester Cathedral. The move was hampered by horrendous storms which lasted for 40 days. Superstitious locals believed they had been cursed by the irritated saint. It is said, that if it rains on 15 July, Saint Swithun's Day, it will continue for 40 days. There is an Elizabethan rhyme:

*Saint Swithun's day if thou dost rain*
*For forty days it will remain.*
*Saint Swithun's day if thou be fair*
*For forty days 'twill rain nae mair.*

## Scala Theatre, Scala Cinema, Angel Place

The Scala was opened as a theatre in 1922 by a consortium of local businessmen. The Scala Theatre was opened as a cinema on 27 November 1922 with 'Theodora'. There was seating in stalls and circle levels. It was independently operated, it was a 'first-run cinema', showing films when it they been just released, The Scala was the first cinema in Worcester to have CinemaScope installed, the CinemaScope screen was installed forward of the original proscenium, reopening on 22 March 1954 with 'The Robe'. The Scala was closed on 2 June 1973 with 'Bequest to a Nation'. The building was gutted internally and became the Worcester Leisure Centre. Since at least 2009, the building has been in use as an amusement arcade.

Next door to the cinema was the Angel Street Corn Exchange building. Built in 1848, this became Worcester's main Corn Exchange until the late 1800s.

## Shire Hall, Foregate Street

Shire Hall was constructed in 1835, to a Grecian design by Charles Day and Henry Rowe. In the foreground is the statue of Queen Victoria, the work of Sir Thomas Brock RA, with her symbolic orb and sceptre. This marble statue, commemorates her Golden Jubilee in 1887. In 1938 Shire Hall became the Worcestershire County Council headquarters.

Presently, it is here that the Crown Court and the County Court sessions are held. The building for the judges is behind the hall. A major refurbishment took place at the Shire Hall which was completed in 1995.

## Shrub Hill Railway Station

The first station at Shrub Hill was opened in 1850, it was jointly owned by the Oxford, Worcester and Wolverhampton Railway and Midland Railway.

The present station building was designed by Edward Wilson and built in 1865. It is a Georgian-style building mainly of engineering brick with stone facings. Originally there was also a train shed which was removed in the 1930s. It is now one of two stations serving the city, managed by London Midland, and served by Great Western.

On platform 2b is the ladies' waiting room (below), a cast-iron structure cast at the Worcester Vulcan Iron Works, manufacturers of railway equipment. This was a subsidiary of the MacKenzie and Holland signal manufacturing company about 200 yards from Worcester Shrub Hill station. The exterior is decorated with classical pilasters

and covered with 'majolica' ceramic tiles made by Maw and Company of Broseley. Maw was originally a Worcester company founded in 1850 when they bought the old Chamberlain tile factory. However in 1852 they moved to Broseley to be nearer their source of clay.

The waiting room is Grade II-listed, the official records state that the waiting room was added in 1880, but placed it on the 'Buildings At Risk Register' in 2003. Finally, restoration was started in 2012.

A second city station, Foregate Street Station, was opened by the Great Western Railway in 1860.

## Silver Cinema, Foregate Street

The Silver Cinema opened in 1915, in a building originally built in 1835 to host the Empire Music Hall, and the Public Library and Hastings Museum. The museum went into serious decline in the 1860s, and eventually the Victoria Institute was built to give it a new home.

By the 1930s, no longer able to compete with custom-built cinemas like the Scala and the Northwick, the Silver Cinema closed and the site was purchased by Oscar Deutsh in 1935, the building was demolished, and a big new cinema was planned.

Unfortunately the outbreak of World War Two saw the building requisitioned, and until 1948 it was home to Spitfire parts, amongst other things.

Eventually, the new Odeon Cinema opened in 1950. The name Odeon comes from 'Oscar Deutsch Entertains Our Nation'.

## Swan Theatre, The Moors

Dame Peggy Ashcroft laid the foundation stone for the Swan Theatre in 1963. It opened its doors for the first time in 1965. Its first production was 'One Wild Oat' in that same year. Two years later John Hole was appointed the first professional artistic director. John was trained in theatre management at the Bernard Miles' Mermaid Theatre, London, in the 1960s. From there he went to the Oxford New Theatre; then to become theatre manager at the Yvonne Arnaud Theatre in Guildford; moving to Worcester in 1967, where he became Theatre Director of the Swan Theatre.

The Swan Theatre, and Huntingdon Hall, are run by Worcester Live. This registered charity is the main arts provider in the city and also runs the annual Shakespeare at the Commandery, Shakespeare at the Cathedral and the Ghost Walks of Worcester.

## Theatre Royal, Angel Street

A theatre stood on this site (now The Co-operative supermarket) as far back as 1780. It became The Theatre Royal in 1884 when the building was bought by a group of amateur actors and rebuilt. This theatre brought down its curtain for the last time on May 28, 1955, was demolished in 1960 and was replaced by a car showroom, then a supermarket. Many famous names trod the boards at the Theatre Royal, names such as:

| | |
|---|---|
| Sarah Siddons | Henry Irving |
| Stan Laurel | Charlie Chaplin |
| Gracie Fields | Julie Andrews |

## Tudor House, Friar Street

Standing in Friar Street, there is a noticeable black and white timber-framed house, with its leaded windows. Inside the 500-year-old rooms have decorated plaster ceilings and walls made of horsehair and dung. Sandstone foundations of this building date back to the 13th century.

In 1550 the building was divided into separate dwellings and used as a place of work for weavers, clothiers, tailors, bakers, painters, and even a lodging house. One of these dwellings, over a period of almost 200 years, was a brewing house and an inn called the Cross Keys.

In the early 1900s the building was bought by the Cadbury family. It became a confectioners, with a tea room upstairs known as the 'Tudor Coffee House'.

In 1921, Tudor House was bought by the Worcester Corporation for use as a school clinic, where many local children came for their inoculations and dental checks. During World War II the building was an ARP (Air Raid Protection) centre and billeting office.

Tudor House was taken over by the Worcester City Museums in 1971. It became known as the Museum of Local Life. It closed down in March 2003 due to budget cuts. Then in April 2004, volunteers known as the 'Worcester Heritage Amenity Trust,' opened part of the ground floor to the public; and by 2006 the whole of Tudor House was re-opened.

Today this building is known as the Tudor House Heritage and Education Centre, with displays of local history, crafts and culture in several rooms, complemented by a shop and coffee rooms serving drinks and cakes. It is open to the public from 10am to 4pm, on Wednesday and Saturday and certain bank holidays. Entrance is free.

Helen Wallis, manageress, told me that the shop was their only source of revenue. During my visit she showed me a beautiful watercolour painting by Maureen Birch, which the artist donated to Tudor House.

Helen introduced me to volunteer worker John Sanders, a retired Marine Motor Engineer with the RNLI, and a model maker. John showed me the hop press, which was in a pitiful state. John told there were very few presses left. This one came from a local hophouse. In the Weaver Room there are hands-on material for children to work with.

## Unicorn Hotel

The Unicorn Hotel, this was one of the principal coaching inns of Georgian Worcester. This Grade II-listed building, built about 1830, now forms part of the shops and offices in Broad Street as it looms over the entrance to the Crowngate Centre. It was one of the main coaching inns of Georgian Worcester.

## University of Worcester

University of Worcester was awarded its current status in 2005 by HM Privy Council. From 1997 it was known as University College Worcester and previous to that it was called Worcester College of Higher Education.

The main campus is known as 'Saint John's'. The University's second campus opened in 2010, is called the 'City Campus' and is home to The Worcester Business School. It is situated on the site of the former Royal Infirmary. Work began there in 2007 and is estimated to have cost over £120 million.

## Victoria Institute, Foregate Street

Victoria Institute is one of Worcester's magnificent buildings. It was especially constructed to house a combined museum, library and school of art and science in time for the jubilee of Queen Victoria. It was built in homage to Queen Victoria after her Golden Jubilee, which she celebrated in 1887. The Duke of York (later to become King George V), laid the foundation stone in April, 1894. In October 1896 this building with its single turret and weather vane, was formerly opened by Lady Mary Lygon, then the Mayoress.

Up until 2012 the front section of the building on Foregate Street was the city's library, museum and art gallery; the rear of Victoria Institute, formally the Museum of Natural History, Geology, and Local Antiquities, was converted into flats in 2001.

In the summer of 2012 the library moved out to become part of The Hive on Sawmill Walk, The Butts.

## Vinegar Factory, Lowesmoor

William Hill and Edward Evans, two chemists, founded their vinegar manufacturing business in Worcester in 1830. They named their company Hill, Evans & Co. and acquired a six-acre site in the Lowesmoor area, on which they built new factory buildings in the 1850s.

For the next century, it was the largest vinegar factory in the world.

At one time they were famous for having the world's largest vat being 40-foot high and able to contain 114,821 gallons. It produced nine million litres (two million gallons) of malt vinegar every year, reputedly some of the finest vinegar in England. The firm grew rapidly, branched into making British wine, sherry and port, as well as quinine, which was drunk to try to combat malaria. And, by 1863, the company also produced blackcurrant, black grape, cherry, champagne, cowslip, elder, ginger, lemon, Madeira, orange, raspberry, raisin, rhubarb, sloe gin, and white currant wine.

The most impressive building is still standing, is Grade II-listed is known as the 'Great Filling Hall'.

As the factory expanded it was found that a link to the railway would be needed. This required new powers to be used that were contained in The Worcester Railways Act, 1870. This Act of Parliament allowed the Company, at their expense, to extend the existing branch line that had one time served The Worcester Engine Works Company, which was linked to the nearby Shrub Hill station by its own branch line. This was from the point where that branch line or siding had crossed the Virgin's Tavern Road (now Tolladine Road) by a further 'two furlongs and nine chains' (632 yards) to terminate in Saint Martin's Street opposite to the northern boundary wall of the vinegar works. This required a level crossing at Shrub Hill Road, a bridge over the Worcester & Birmingham Canal, and another level crossing at Pheasant Street. The whole branch line from the Worcester engine shed yard to the vinegar works was completed in 1872, and became known as the Vinegar Works Branch. By 1902 the brewery buildings covered about seven acres, with an extensive network of underground vaults.

Hill Evans & Co. was manufacturing up until 1965.

The transformation of the former vinegar works was part of the £75 million project to revitalise Lowesmoor. The area has been taken over by the Saint Martin's Quarter development. 'The Great Filling Hall', now named Dancox House, has been converted to become the Territorial Army's local training centre and headquarters and a high-quality business centre. The building which has been named after Private Frederick Dancox, of Dolday, was the city's only born and bred winner of the Victoria Cross.

## Walls Around the City

The monastery and cathedral were defended by a citadel wall, built by 1224, and constructed of red sandstone, although some were green, from quarries at Holt and Ombersley. The main entrance being on the site of the Edgar Tower.

An original motte and bailey castle was built around 1069 by Urse d'Abetot who was the first Norman sheriff of the county. The motte of the castle was levelled some time between 1820 and 1840 and today the King's School occupies the site but Severn Street still follows the line of the former moat. During the reign of King John, all the land that had been appropriated by Sheriff Urso was restored back to the Monks.

The Grade II-listed walls are one of many highlighted by English Heritage. James Dunn, who is the City Council archaeological officer, stated that the council faced a tough challenge co-ordinating almost thirty different land owners to carry out repairs to the walls. He is quoted as saying:

*'If you look at the city wall there are some bits which are in need of some fairly urgent attention and some of it is not in a very presentable condition. What we really have to do is try and work in partnership with the owners, talk to them nicely and try and provide them with grant aid along with English Heritage to make sure thy would be able to do carry out repairs without excessive cost to themselves.*

There were five towers and gates in the city wall:

1. Foregate tower and gate, leading to the North.
2. Saint Martin's tower and gate leading to the East.
3. Friar's tower and gate also leading to the East.
4. Sidbury tower and gate leading South.
5. Water Gate (Saint Clement Gate near old bridge) the only surviving gate.

Work to piece back together parts of Worcester's ancient city walls started in 2011. Specialist stonemasons had been commissioned to repair and clean up the city's mediaeval sandstone defences as part of a joint project between Worcester City Council, English Heritage and the National Trust.

### Whitehouse Hotel, Foregate Street

This Hotel was originally called the Star Hotel. Before that it was a coaching inn, and today one can still see the large archway running from the front to back. The hotel took its name from the star of cap badge of the Worcestershire Regiment.

It was here, in 1865, that the Worcestershire Cricket Club was formed, with Lord Lyttleton elected as president. It was also where, for 16 years, the Worcester Boxing Club was based.

### Worcester's Bathing Barges

In 1910, these barges, were moored alongside Pitchcroft and used by hundreds of people. Charles Albert Webb was attendant for the men's swimming barge; his pay being one guinea per week.

Eunice Soden was the attendant for the ladies' bathing barge with a salary of £1 per week, which included assistance given by her grandfather, Charles Webb.

*Worcester Bridge, 18th century engraving*

### Worcester Bridge

The first bridge across the River Severn was constructed in wood in 1299. A stone bridge across the River Severn was completed in 1318.

The centre arch of this bridge was damaged in the Civil War. It was rebuilt in 1662. A few years later the bridge was very badly damaged by ice during extremely cold winters.

A new stone bridge, designed by John Gwynn RA, was opened in 1781, together with a toll-house. The first toll was paid by William Broughton, who also paid the very last toll. On that Opening Day in 1781, there was much celebrating; several small cannons were firing and church bells were ringing.

In 1809 the toll charge to cross Worcester Bridge on foot was lifted.

By 1841 the traffic had increased considerably and the River Severn Engineer Edward Leader Williams designed a cast iron footpath, with iron balustrade, to span the river each side of the main bridge for pedestrians to use. In 1847, this cast-iron footpath was added making Worcester Bridge wider. This graceful structure survived until the 1930s when it was decided to widen each side of Gwynne's bridge with stonework. This would make the bridge three times wider and that the ironwork would be sent to the scrap heap.

In 1932 Elgar's friend Billy Reed wrote:

*'One day when I arrived at Marl Bank, Elgar's last home on Rainbow Hill, I was rushed off to see what they were doing at Worcester, widening the bridge over his beloved Severn, the old familiar bridge he had known all his life.*

*I was taken there so often that I guessed he had something in his head about it.*

*At last it came out – he could not bear to part with the old iron balustrades that were being removed; so he bought two lengths of them and had them brought up on lorries to Marl Bank and set up there on a concrete bed.'*

Marl Bank was demolished in 1969, a block of flats, Elgar Court, stands in its place. A local enthusiast salvaged the ironwork.

In 1932, Worcester Bridge was reconstructed, and it was reopened by Edward, Prince of Wales on 28 October 1932.

## Worcester Cathedral

There has been a cathedral in Worcester since the 7th century, the first cathedral was constructed in wood in 680AD, with Bishop Bosel at its head.

The Worcester Cathedral of today, with its 196ft tower, dominating the river and the bridge along the Severn, was begun by Saint Wulstan, Bishop of Worcester, in 1084, after the Norman Conquest. Its original title was 'The Cathedral Church of Christ and the Blessed Mary the Virgin of Worcester'.

The Cathedral suffered a major fire in 1113 and a second in 1147. When King Stephen visited the Cathedral in 1139, he gave a ring, which he placed on the High Altar; in that same year it became a sanctuary for citizens when forces of the Empress

Matilda attacked the city.

In 1158, King Henry II and his wife visited Worcester and placed their crowns on the altar, and vowed that they would never wear them again.

When Bishop Wulstan was canonised in 1203, there was another fire. A gigantic restoration programme took place in 1218, and. King Henry III came for the re-consecration of the Cathedral. Its many attractions include:

*Worcester Cathedral, from 'A Survey of Worcester', Valentine Green, 1764*

The Nave which is mostly 14th century. The westerly bays are late Norman.

The north and south aisles contain monuments from the 15th to 19th centuries.

The Pulpit is by Sir Gilbert Scott.

The large west window is by Hardman, dated 1874.

The Lady Chapel is a very decorative part with its purbeck marble shafts and sculpture dating back to the 13th century.

The Crypt, the largest Norman crypt in England, is approached through a modern entrance from the south choir aisle, and is a fine example of early Norman work.

Chapter House is 12th century and one of the most famous works of art of mediaeval England.

Edward Elgar's plaque and window.

The Bishop's throne.

The Jesus Chapel.

The High Altar with King John's tomb of 1216; a carved effigy of him created from purbeck marble.

*The stonework remains of Guesten Hall, built in 1320 for the cathedral's monks to offer hospitality to strangers and guests, was mostly demolished in 1862, but one large side wall with its four window voids survived. The remains were carefully repaired in 2011, after a £250,000 three-year project involving skilled stonemasons.*

The Mediaeval Cloisters; a Norman crypt with Pilgrim exhibition. Prince Arthur's Chantry, eldest son of Henry VII.

Saint Wulstan's Crypt.

Saint George's Chapel with 'Woodbine Willie' memorial.

The Victorian stained glass and the Wilde monument.

The Cloisters are well worth a visit, with its very beautiful 14th century passages, linking Worcester Cathedral with College Green, through an impressive Norman archway.

In February, 2008, the cathedral was given the sum of £140,000, from English Heritage, to help finance a £10m restoration project, which started in 1988, and is now completed. Out of the nine cathedrals in this country, Worcester is the only one that employs its own team of stonemasons for restoration work.

### Worcester Royal Infirmary

Known as the Charles Hasting Building, it was built on a plot of land purchased on Castle Street to build a hospital to solve the increasing problem of limited beds at the earlier Silver Street Infirmary. When the first Infirmary was opened in Worcester at Silver Street in 1746, it was a voluntary hospital, established for the working classes associated with the city's industry. The very poorest of society had access to healthcare through the infirmaries attached to the workhouses of the time. 'Voluntary' referred to the method of funding the hospital, through voluntary subscriptions. As soon as the Silver Street Infirmary opened it became apparent that the provision of beds was not going to be enough. A new hospital building would have to be built. Two acres of land in Artichoke Field were purchased in 1765 and Anthony Keck won the competition to build the new hospital in the following year.

The new infirmary was a classical style designed by Keck, the masons were recorded as Bowen Stephens and Bott and the carpenter was Edward Haskow. Building work began in 1768 with red bricks made on Pitchcroft, but suffered setbacks due to unreliable builders, floods on Pitchcroft, and funds running out. Overcoming obstacles, the new Infirmary was opened and occupied on 17 September 1770 with the final patients being transferred the following year.

It was in this building, in 1832, at a meeting in the board room held by Charles Hastings, the Provincial Medical and Surgical Association was founded, which was later to become the British Medical Association (BMA).

*The neo-Norman chapel, now the Jenny Lind Chapel*

A Neo-Norman chapel was added in 1850 by Henry Day, which started a string of improvements and additions over the next twenty years. In 1866 the railings from the Worcester Arboretum were moved here to be sited on the north and east sides.

*The new stained glass window in the Jenny Lind Chapel, designed by local artist Nick Upton, made by Rob Paddock of the Art of Glass at Burcott Forge, unveiled by Henry Sandon MBE, and was paid for by the Worcester Royal Infirmary Nurses' League. It is a memorial to the those who worked at the hospital and in special memory of Edna Butler.*

The former Infirmary has been transformed into an establishment of higher education. In September 2010, the new city campus of the University of Worcester was opened to students and staff, giving a new, 21st Century purpose to such a beautiful building. It is home to the Worcester Business School, the former wards, domestic rooms, and offices have been

*Work to transform the former Infirmary into an establishment of higher education began in 2008, completed and opened in September 2010*

sympathetically converted to light, contemporary teaching spaces with wireless networks and modern digital technology.

As a further tribute to the history of its past, a £537,000 grant from the Heritage Lottery Fund was used to establish a new interactive museum of medical history within the former Infirmary, in partnership with the original George Marshall Medical Museum at the Worcestershire Royal Hospital. Schools, families and the wider community are welcome to visit both museums and enjoy learning more about medical history. The Museum in the Charles Hastings Education Centre at the Worcestershire Royal Hospital and the new museum on the ground floor of the Charles Hastings Building, accessed from Infirmary Walk, are open Monday to Friday 10am – 4pm.

### Worcestershire Royal Hospital

The Worcestershire Royal Hospital in Charles Hastings Way opened in March 2002. It replaced the ageing Worcester Royal Infirmary in Castle Street and the former Ronkswood Hospital. It provides 550 patient beds, includes nine operating theatres, a large Accident and Emergency Department and Critical Care Unit, and specialist radiology and scanning facilities, in 38,000 square metres.

### Worcester Woods, Worcester Countryside Centre

The is the first accredited Country Park in England, Worcester Woods has 100 acres of ancient Oak woodland. Many Ancient trees can be found in Nunnery Wood, an indication of its ancient standing. The ancient Oak on the edge of the woods is well over 500 years old. It has been left to mark the boundary of the wood.

The Woods are alive with bluebells in spring, woodland birds, wildflower meadows, bees and butterflies feeding on the sweet nectar in early summer. Alongside is enough wide open space to let off steam, fly a kite, kick a ball or exercise the dog.

The woodland pond also attracts a wide variety of wildlife. Dragonflies, frogs, great-crested newts and many other plants and insects thrive in and around the water.

Hornhill Meadows have been meadows since mediaeval times making them particularly valuable for their wild flowers. The meadows attract clouds of butterflies in the summer months like the common blue, meadow brown, small copper and gatekeeper. The meadows are mown later than modern hay crops to allow flowers to spread their seeds for next year. They are also lightly grazed during occasional winters, most recently by rare breeds of long horn cattle, to help remove nutrients and keep the grasses from taking over. Look too for the fruit of the old pear trees in the hedges, a traditional symbol of Worcestershire.

The Countryside Centre includes a cafe, information point, a couple of seminar rooms and plenty of ideas for entertaining the children. On the flag pole flies the 'Green Flag award'.

An area of orchard, the only remains of Horn Hill Farm dating back to the early 19th century, has recently been restored.

## Workhouses

From 1834 to 1930, the only sanctioned method of dealing with the poor in this England was by putting them in workhouses. There were many workhouses in Worcester, all of which have now been demolished. These included: All Saints parish workhouse, Dolday, near North Quay, in 1930; Worcester Union Workhouse, Foregate, in 1888 and Saint Nicholas Workhouse, Saint Peters Road, in 1898.

A new workhouse was erected in 1888, on Tallow Hill, designed by George Byfield. In 1894 this workhouse was completely rebuilt. An article in the Worcester Herald, 22 April 1893, stated that there had been some disagreement amongst the Guardians as to whether a ceremony should be held, Mrs Browne, felt that there was nothing to celebrate in the erection of such a horrible building, it was rather a matter to be despised; and whether the erection of a workhouse was really necessary.

However, a ceremony did take place for the new workhouse and a foundation stone was laid, on which it reads:

> THIS FOUNDATION STONE
> WAS LAID BY MISS BELLERS
> DAUGHTER OF COLONEL R B BELLERS J.P.
> CHAIRMAN OF THE BOARD OF GUARDIANS
> 18th MAY 1893

### Ye Old Talbot Inn, Sidbury

The Old Talbot Inn was originally the Church House for Saint Michael's. It stood in the Cathedral churchyard, and dated back to the 13th century. This inn played an important role in the baking of bread and also in the brewing of ales for church occasions; it also had ten lodging chambers as well as stabling.

After the Civil War the Old Talbot Inn became the 'Court Inn'. In 1966, it underwent modernisation during which time Saxon human remains were found. This inn is now owned by Flower & Sons Limited, a member of the Whitbread Group since 1926.

### On the outskirts of Worcester
### The Mug House Inn

This ancient pub is unique, it is one of only two pubs that stand on consecrated ground. This one time church brew house was built in the fifteenth century, possibly rebuilt, later altered and enlarged during mid-nineteenth century and re-modelled mid-twentieth century. It has an history that goes back to the time of the Plantagenets and the House of Lancaster.

Brew houses were at one time an essential form of income for the church for with some 75 feast days to celebrate it meant money for the coffers of the church. But, as with all church alehouses it came under scrutiny by the Puritans who closed most of the ale houses because of the drunken and lewd behaviour of the population at the time. The Mug House survived.

In modern times an external wall was damaged during a violent storm, when repairs were being carried out a silver head of a Bishops Crosier was found in the wall. Later investigations revealed that it once belonged to the Bishop of Worcester; but why was it there? And, when was it placed there, by whom? A real mystery. The crosier is now used by the Boy Bishop.

The Mug House is also known to be haunted, things move about in the cellar when the licensee is attending to the barrels, a mallet is mysteriously moved from one side of the cellar to the other, doors open and close without apparent cause. This has been put down to that of a mischievous child.

# Chapter four
## Worcester streets

How some of our Worcester streets evolved and may have got their names is a very interesting subject. Generally, the word 'street' comes from the Latin word strata (paved Roman road). 'Wich' refers to bays, where salt is found. Four of the most common names for roads and tracks of Roman origin were: Broad Way, Hollow Way, Ridge Way, Salt Way.

In earlier times, street names usually derived from names of local landowners or very important land tenants. The distinction between a street or a lane derived from how wide or narrow it was.

It was normal practice for mediaeval street names to reflect their function, or the economic activity taking place within them, especially the commodities available for sale.

### All Saints Road
This road in the heart of the city is named after All Saints Church on Deansway, an evangelical Anglican church with twelve bells in its bell tower.

### Angel Street
Running off Foregate Street we have Angel Street, taking its name from The Angel Hotel which had extended right through to Broad Street.

In 1638, this street had a bubonic plague pit (claiming 1,551 victims), on the site of what was once a sheep market.

### Arboretum Road
The word 'arboretum' means a collection of trees and shrubs for ornamental purposes, such as a park area. In the 1700s this area was known as Sansome Fields. A villa was built here and the expanse around it was a public park. In 1886 the land was sold for the purpose of building houses.

### Beauchamp Road
This road was named after the powerful Beauchamp family, who appear to have been the patrons of the Friars of Worcestershire.

### Blockhouse Close
This area was once open countryside known as Blockhouse Fields. It became heavily built up in the 19th century, with cottages and factories. 'The Blockhouse' was that part of Worcester that lay roughly down the backs of the properties on the east side of Friar Street. It was extra-parochial, so unmarried mothers-to-be

were apt to be dragged there so that their babies didn't become a charge on the ratepayers of whatever parish the unfortunate woman happened to be living in. Here once stood Sigley's sweet factory and the premises of E H Quinton.

## Brewery Walk

May be reference to the first large scale brewery in Worcester, Britannia Brewery at Barbourne, which was built in 1850. In 1886, it was taken over by Spreckley Brothers Ltd. who were brewers as well as wine merchants. The Spreckley family operated the brewery until 1968.

## Bridge Street

A new bridge over the River Severn was built in 1781, and at the same time Bridge Street was built. To construct this roadway to the bridge, a row of houses, extending from top of Newport Street to the top of Quay Street, was pulled down.

## Broad Street

Was originally a wide market area set aside for the sale of cattle.

## Carden Street

This street was named after Thomas Carden (1738–1836), who became a magistrate and served as Mayor of Worcester in 1790. For many years he was Governor of the *Guardians of the Poor*, he was in public office for 50 years.

## Castle Street

Originally this street was known as Salt Lane, a county gaol (above), designed by Francis Sandys was built 1809–1813, it closed in 1928, was used as temporary accommodation for the homeless of the city, the facade was demolished in the 1930s, but several cells remained until 1987 when they were finally demolished. Its castellated appearance led to the re-naming of Salt Lane.

## Church Street

Church Street was previously known as Dish Market, where the crockery trade took place on every market day.

## City Walls Road

When this road was constructed, it was named after the wall that surrounded the city. For a rough idea as to how the City Wall surrounded the City, start from:

Foregate (along into Sansome Street).
Saint Martin's Gate (via city Walls Road).
Sidbury Gate (principal mediaeval entrance to City).
Edgar Tower Gate (going south of College Green).
Saint Clement's Gate (going around the Cathedral).
Trinity Gate (to Nash's Passage).
Friars Gate (to Sidbury).
Water Gate, (along the river to the Butts).

## College Street

This street, which led to the King's School, was created in 1794. It was widened in the 1960s to form a dual-carriageway continuation of Sidbury, which in the late 1940s had been a horrendous bottleneck.

## Copenhagen Street

This street was renamed in honour of Lord Horatio Nelson's visit to Worcester in 1802. He had been involved in the Battle of Copenhagen the previous year, had led the engagement which saw the British fleet defeating the Danish-Norwegian fleet which was anchored off Copenhagen.

The street was previously known as Cooken Street, a name which is connected with the ducking stool. Ducking-stools and cucking-stools were chairs formerly used for punishment.

The 'The Mouth of the Nile' inn, in Copenhagen Street, was another reference to one of Nelson's victorious battle scenes. Nelson led a defeat against a large French convoy led by Napoleon Bonaparte.

## Coventry Avenue and Croome Road

Named after connections of George William (1722–1809), the 6th Earl of Coventry. He served as Lord Lieutenant of Worcestershire between 1751 to 1808. In 1752 he brought in Lancelot 'Capability' Brown's for the landscape design of Croome Court he had just inherited.

## Cripplegate

Originally the word 'crypel-geat' referred to a low opening in the fence or wall, allowing sheep to pass through.

## Cross, The

This street was named after a cross of mediaeval times which dominated the area. The Cross became the main commercial trading street of the city.

## Dent Street

This street refers to John Dent (1757–1855) who established his accessory company, manufacturing fine leather gloves, Dent Allcroft and Co Ltd. It was founded in a timbered cottage in 1777. By 1814, he was a prominent member of the '48' of the Corporation of Worcester. In 1823. He served as Chamberlain, and in 1824, held the position of High Sheriff of the County in 1849. John Dent was elected Mayor of Worcester in 1826.

## Diglis Lane

The word 'diglis' comes from Norman French 'D'Eglise' meaning 'of the church', which may be a reference that these lands were some of the first to be given to the Priory.

## Dolday

The Dolday, a corruption of a Norman term meaning 'dole of God' runs down from The Butts toward the river. The corner house was where the Friars' bakehouse stood, and where 'doles' were given out. The word 'doles' refers to a share of charitable money, food or clothing given away. The Dolday was largely occupied by people associated with the cloth industry. By the 18th century it had fallen into decline, today only the lower part of the street exists.

## Droitwich Road

This was the 'salt road' leading from Droitwich to Salt Lane (now called Castle Street) in Worcester.

Salt was transported to a distribution centre where it could be sold to centres accessible by the waterways. In Roman times when Droitwich was just a village, it was called Salinae (the salt pans), and was located at the junction of several Roman roads. Rock salt and brine was extracted in Droitwich.

In the mid-19th century, Droitwich became famous as a Spa town, its brine baths opened in 1830, but unfortunately closed in 2008 after health and safety inspections. SOBBS (Save Our Brine Baths) is working hard with BMI Healthcare to reopen the baths.

## Edgar Street

This street (formerly known as Knowles End) was named after King Edgar the Peacemaker (AD 943–975), who took over Mercia and Northumbria even before he became the King of the English in 959 to 975AD.

## Fish Street

This street was named after the fish market that once took place here. It was known as Corviser Street in mediaeval times and was occupied by cordwainers or leather-workers.

At the west end of this street stands Saint Alban's, the smallest church in the City.

The definition of the mediaeval word 'Corviser' derives from the old French word for 'shoemaker'.

*The Farriers Arms, in Fish Street, previously known as 'The Globe and The Dark Angel' is one of the oldest public houses in Worcester. The building was originally two houses before being converted into a public house. It is 17th century and grade II-listed*

## Foregate Street

The original word 'fordget' of 1170. referred to a tract of land in front of the city gate. Many of the houses in Foregate Street are over 300 years old, belonging to the rich citizens and the professional men, some of these houses had stables and coach houses.

The Fore Gate, which was part of the City Wall, which stood close to the Hop Market Hotel, was demolished in 1651.

In the early part of the 19th century, the mother of the Princess Victoria (later to become Queen) brought her daughter to Worcester to see the Cathedral. They had lunch at the Hop Pole Hotel (on the corner of Shaw Street and Foregate Street).

As the crowd gathered at the hotel entrance, in anticipation of the Royal visitors' arrival, a fight broke out, involving a number of people, and just as Princess Victoria was arriving. It was a very dangerous moment, but the incident promoted the hotel to be re-named Victoria House.

## Friar Street

Friar Street was built up in 1331, and is largely unchanged. It is one of the very few streets where it's still possible to appreciate the mediaeval period.

A house of Augustinian Friars was founded in Droitwich in 1331. Franciscan friars were known as Greyfriars because of the colour of their robes, Dominican friars were called Blackfriars because of their black cloaks, and arrived in Worcester in 1347.

Most of the buildings in Friar Street go back to the 16th and 17th century, they stand proudly in varying degrees of lean.

Friar Street gives much pleasure to the many thousands of tourists that come to visit this lovely City.

## Hamilton Road

William Hamilton, second Duke of Hamilton, was the son of James, Second Marquis of Hamilton. There is a memorial brass and bronze tablet at Worcester Cathedral to William, who, at the age of 34, was in command of the Royalist forces at Fort Royal. William Hamilton died at the Commandery, as the result of serious wounds that he received in the historical fight against Cromwell on 3 September, 1651.

## Hebb Street

This street got its name from Christopher Henry Hebb (1772–1849) who was practicing the art of healing in Worcester. Hebb was elected Mayor of Worcester in 1836, serving for two years. In his will he bequeathed £5 a year, to be given away at Christmas through the purchase of bread, which was to be distributed amongst the poor, residing in the Tything of Whistones, and the district of Saint George's, South Claines.

## High Street

Ten centuries ago the word 'high' meant something excellent or superior, and was applied to roads as they improved their status, becoming the focal point for shops and commerce in city centres. In 1978, this street became a pedestrianised shopping area.

## King Street

Named because Charles II passed along it after leaving the Commandery, during his escape t the Battle of Worcester.

## Lansdowne Road

This road was once known as 'Cut Throat Lane,' taking its name from a favourite duelling spot, known as Rogers Hill. Later, the road was named after Bevil Grenville (1596–1643). Grenville was a Royalist commander in the English Civil War. He won a battle at Lansdowne Hill, outside the city of Bath, which gave the road its current name.

## Laslett Street

The street is named after William Laslett (1801–1884), who was born in Worcester. He practiced for many years as a solicitor at Number 50 Foregate Street. In 1842 he married Maria, eldest daughter of Doctor Carr, the Bishop of Worcester.

William Laslett was a Liberal MP for Worcester (1852 to 1860). Later he became a Conservative MP for Worcester from 1868 to 1874.

## Lich Street

This was an ancient street, named after the Lychgate (a covered gateway where the coffins were rested before entry to the graveyard), linking the High Street with Sidbury. Lich Street was demolished during a programme of redevelopment in the 1960s. It was one of the city's oldest surviving backwaters. By the last century it had became a poor quarter, populated by working class folk and full of 'common lodging houses.'

## Lydiate

This was spelt Lidyate in 1343. It was a gate that led into the forest of Ombersley from the Worcester-Droitwich road.

## Lyttelton Street

This street was named after George William Lyttelton (1817–1876), who was Mr Gladstone's brother-in-law.

## Mealcheapen Street

This street was previously called the Cornmarket. For centuries this was the commercial centre of the city, where corn was the main commodity on sale.

At the bottom of Mealcheapen Street is the Cornmarket Square, where once stood the Public Hall, demolished in 1996, replaced by a car park. Well into the 19th century, this street was a place of punishment where the stocks and pillory stood, and where public whippings took place. In earlier times a gallows stood in this market, where severed limbs were often put on display.

## Nash's Passage

This post-mediaeval alleyway, off New Street, is named after John Nash (1590–1662), who was the son of John and Isobel Nash of Ripperidge.

Nash House in New Street, which still stands today, is a Grade II-listed building built in 1605 for John's father, Richard Nash, who died that same year; he left the house to his son John. John Nash became an alderman and a noted Worcester benefactor.

## New Road

This road came into being in the 1600s. It leads from Worcester Bridge to Saint John's. New road is the site of the County Cricket Ground, which was created in 1899. It has many memories, but in one historic match, Don Bradman made 236 runs in 1930.

## Perdiswell Street

This street which goes back to 1884, is named after a Saxon well.

## Powick Lane (now Bank Street)

This lane took its name from the Powick Family who lived in Worcester in 1275 and 1327.

## Providence Street

William Blizzard Williamson began a small business manufacturing a range of items in sheet steel and tin plate, pioneering the method of Japanning.

In 1858, he built a factory, called the 'Providence Works' in the Blockhouse, off City Walls Road. William Blizzard died in 1878, leaving the company to his two sons, William and George, who developed the company's products. William developed the 'lever lid' tin, still used today for products like paint and custard powder; while George invented the 'cutter lid tin' for cigarettes and tobacco. The company eventually evolved into the international company Metal Box.

## Pump Street

Pump Street, formerly Nelderstrete, was named after the needle-makers who worked here in 1406. From earliest times, people of Worcester obtained water from wells which were common in the area we know today as the High Street. Water pumps near by, gave the street its name.

This street has been the hub of the Wesleyan and Methodist tradition for over 200 years. Five different Methodist Chapels have graced the same site.

The first to be built was in nearby New Street in 1772, and was visited by the great John Wesley himself, who was very fond of the City of Worcester.

In 1795, the Wesleyans moved to an old chapel building in Pump Street, tucked away up an alley, so as not to invite trouble from angry mobs.

Shortly after, this Wesleyian chapel was replaced by a new chapel. In 1812, more land was bought in Pump Street, and an even larger chapel was built. This chapel was pulled down in 1901 to make way for yet another chapel which survived until 1965, when it closed its doors.

## Quay Street

Severn Trow Public House was an old waterman's inn in Quay Street. The word 'trow' refers to a type of cargo boat that was found on the River Severn; the mast could be taken down so that the trow could go under bridges. the street was named after the wharf (quay) nearby.

## Rowley Hill Street

The street was named after Thomas Rowley Hill, son of the founder of Hill, Evans & Company which manufactured some of the finest vinegar in England.

Rowley Hill Street is on the A44, as you climb the hill out of Worcester. Nearby is Red Hill, where executions took place. Father Edward Oldcome, Ralph Ashley, a tenant farmer called Perkes, Humphrey Littleton and John Wintour were hung, drawn and quartered in 1606, because of their involvement in the 'Gunpowder Plot.' Red Hill is also mentioned in 1651, when Cromwell's forces. attacked the Royalists.

## Saint Paul's Street

This street was previously known as 'Withy Walk,' named after the withy (willow) trees that grew either side of a stream (Worcester Canal). It was later called Spring Hill. It was renamed Saint Paul's Street, after Saint Paul's Church, which was completed in 1887.

Saint Paul's Church is one of the few remaining Victorian buildings in the Blockhouse area, and is well-known for its association with the Reverend G. A. Studdert-Kennedy, otherwise known as 'Woodbine Willy'.

## Saint Peter's Street

This street was originally Church Street. It was renamed Saint Peter's Street, after the mediaeval church of Saint Peter the Great (demolished in 1835).

## Saint Swithin's Street

This street is named after Saint Swithin's (Saint Swithun's) Church. The street was formerly called Goose Lane, (once a market for poultry.

## Salt Lane, now Castle Street

Salt from Droitwich brine reservoirs had been transported to Worcester via the River Severn and traded in Worcester since before Roman times. The merchants, to avoid the toll payable if salt entered the City, made a road across the fields, now Pitchcroft, leading to the Severn, where salt was loaded on to the barges for further exportation. Castle Street was known as Salt Lane until the 19th century.

This street became Castle Street, named after the county gaol, built in 1813, with its castle-like structure.

Public hangings took place at the county gaol until 1863. Edward Corbett of Lea & Perrins Ltd, Worcester, tells the following story:

*'Two old witches lived in Salt Lane. There in front of their cottage was thick deep mud that never seemed to go away. Quite often the salt wagons with their team of horses, would get imbedded in the mud, be unable to move. When this happened, one of the witches would come out of the cottage and offer to help.*

*The wagoner would then offer her sixpence, and then she would stroke the horses and bless them. Immediately the team would pull the wagon out of the deep mud, and continue on its way.*

*One day a wagoner arrived, and got stuck. He had often payed the witch sixpence in previous trips; but on this occasion he thought, with his lighter load, that he would get through the thick mud without the help of the witch. However, he got stuck fast.*

*The witch came out and once again offered to help. But he still insisted that he didn't need any help and jumped on the lead horse and endeavoured to get the wagon moving.*

*It was then, that he spotted a sheaf of straw, caught up in the harness of the horses. He pulled out his knife and cut the straw away. Immediately the horses became frantic and with hooves flying, both the team and wagon went crashing down the lane.*

*Left behind in the lane, could be seen the body of the other witch, cut in half, lying in a pool of blood.'*

## Sandys Road

There have been a few notable 'Sandys' during the history of Worcester. Edwin Sandys (1519–1588) was a learned but quarrelsome man during the reign of Queen Elizabeth I. In 1559 he was appointed Bishop of Worcester (1559–1570). Sir Edwin Sandys (1561–1629), one of the sons of the previous Edwin Sandys, born in Worcester, was an English politician who sat in the House of Commons. Sir Samuel Sandys (1615–1685), great grandson of the first Edwin Sandys, was an English politician who sat in the House of Commons at various times between 1640 and 1685, he fought for the Royalists in the English Civil War. Samuel Sandys, 1st Baron Sandys

(1695–1770), son of the second Edwin Sandys, was a British politician, MP for Worcester. Edwin Sandys, 2nd Baron Sandys (1726–1797), the eldest son of Samuel Sandys, was a British politician, MP for Droitwich.

## Severn Street

This street (formerly Frog Mill Lane, then Frog Lane, and afterwards High Timber Street), runs from Edgar Street down to the River Severn.

Severn Street follows the line of the castle ditch. The castle, which was an earth and timber fortress (later strengthened by stone walls), was built by the Normans in the 1060s. This castle site is now occupied by King's School.

## The Shambles

'Shambles' was the name originally used for a street of butchers shops where meat was slaughtered and sold. It comes from a middle English word: 'schamel', which means a bench (or the Anglo-saxon 'scamel' a stool) and refered to merchants who kept a stall or bench for meat, fruit, vegetables etc., in the street or market.

And, The Shambles did have, at one time, seventeen butchers' shops, many of which had their own slaughter house. After 9 o'clock on a Saturday night butchers would endeavour to auction off their unsold meat cheaply, bearing in mind there wasn't any refrigeration in those days of the early 1900s.

Crowds of poor people would gather round the shops waiting for a bargain piece of meat, with shops staying open until 10pm.

## Shaw Street

This street is named after William Shaw (1766–1843) a leather seller who was residing at number 7 Mealcheapen Street. In 1821, he served as sheriff, and two years later he became Mayor of Worcester.

## Sheriff Street

Alexander Clunes Sherriff was one of the most important Victorians in Worcester. He was already well established before being brought to Worcester in the 1850s to revitalise the fortunes of the Oxford Worcester & Wolverhampton Railway (OW&WR) (by this time the railway was so run down its customers named it the 'Old Worse & Worse'). Under Sheriff's leadership things improved so much that by 1863 it was sold to the Great Western Railway. Sheriff then formed the Worcester Engine Works Co. Ltd with amongst others Walter Holland. Sheriff went on to become the MP for Worcester, Chairman of Worcester Porcelain Co, a director of several railways in London and of a Russian steelworks. Sheriff became Mayor of Worcester from 1862 to 1863

## Silver Street

In this street once stood a silversmith. There was also a bell foundry (until 1774), run by John Martin the elder, where many church bells were cast. John Martin's bells are quite numerous and are also found in Warwickshire and Herefordshire. Worcester had a long tradition of bellfounding from mediaeval times through to the mid-1690s when the foundries of John Martin the younger were in full swing.

## Somers Road

This road is named after John Somers, 1st Baron Somers, PC, FRS (1651–1716), born in Claines, and was the eldest son of John Somers, an attorney in Worcester. John Somers was Defence Council at the trial of the Seven Bishops. John Somers was made Solicitor-General, and was the confidential adviser to William III. John Somers became Lord Chancellor of England (1697) under King William III.

## Spring Lane

Natural springs were discovered and tapped at the foot of Tallow Hill, the Spring Gardens and Spring Lane area providing Worcester with an opportunity to exploit the 18th century rage for 'taking the waters',

## Stallard Road

The earliest record of the Stallard family's wine-trade connection in Worcester is Thomas Stallard supplying sacramental wine to the Cathedral in the reign of Henry V11. The firm of Josiah Stallard and Sons was founded in 1808 when William Stallard (1777–1855) took over the wine business of Mary and Lucy Hooper, trading from the vaulted cellars and extensive premises bordered by High Street, Copenhagen Street and Fish Street, he was a member of the '48' of Worcester City Corporation in 1824 until 1835.

William Stallard was also elected a councillor for All Saints' Ward in the reformed Council in 1836.

Malpas Stallard Limited continues trading to this day, in Fish Street, as traditional wine merchants, offering experienced, personal service to a loyal wholesale and retail clientele.

## Trinity Street

This street is named after the Trinity Hospital, school and almshouses that once stood here. All that remains is the 15th century galleried timber-framed Queen Elizabeth House.

## Vernon Park Road

A street named after any one of the many fortunes of the Vernon family; from their beginnings as the Elizabethan rectors of Hanbury parish, the Vernons rose to become one of the most prominent families in Worcestershire. The Vernon family history is well-documented at Hanbury Hall.

Thomas Vernon (1654–1721) amassed a fortune as an eminent Chancery barrister for 40 years, as well as becoming Whig MP for Worcester in 1715, in the first parliament of George I.

## Wakeman Street

In 1801, Perdiswell was described as the elegant seat of Henry Wakeman, on whom a baronetcy was conferred upon him in 1828. There is a bust of him in Claines Church. Henry Wakeman died in 1831.

His Grandson, also named Henry was a retired manufacturer, and was Deputy Lieutenant, lived the life of a country gentleman. He lent his grounds for the gathering of public assemblies, etc.

## Warmstry Court

Near this Court was once 'Warmstry Slip' (Saint Mary's Lane) near Worcester Bridge. The new Royal Worcester Porcelain factory was at Warmstry House, once the home of the Warmstry family.

## Waterworks Road

This road is named after the City Waterworks which was built in 1858 (to replace the old elevated waterworks of 1795, that stood at the top of Pitchcroft). Unfiltered water was pumped from the river into a reservoir on Rainbow Hill. It was not until 1894 that water was filtered, resulting in an almost immediate drop in typhoid cases.

## White Ladies Close

This Close, is named after the 'White Ladies', referring to the nuns who wore white habits and who lived at the White Ladies Priory, or Priory of Saint Leonard at Brewood, now in ruins, in the parish of Boscobel, Shropshire. Charles II hid nearby in 1651, before moving to Boscobel House, during the English Civil War.

## Wood Terrace

Wood Street is named after Miss Ellen Price (1814–1887), eldest daughter of Thomas Price, who inherited from his father, William Price, a glove manufacturing business in Worcester City.

In 1836, Ellen Price married Henry Wood, who was a prominent member of a banking and shipping firm. Ellen Wood travelled abroad, mainly in Europe.

In 1861, her first book 'East Lynne'

was published, it became a well-known stage play. She went on to write many novels under the pen-name of Johnny Ludlow, including:

'A life's Sonnet'
'The Channings'
'Mrs Halliburton's Troubles'.

Ellen Wood was very much in love with Worcestershire and its history and often reproduced it in her books.

For example, in one of her short stories called 'A Day in Malvern,' Ellen relates a frightening scene from a true account. In 1826, a group of young people were sheltering from a nasty violent storm. They were huddled together in Lady Harcourt Tower, on one of the Malvern Hills; when the tower was struck by lightning and four of them died.

## Wylde's Lane

Is named after Thomas Wylde (1508–1560), son of Simon Wylde. Thomas Wylde, a cloth maker, bought the Commandery in 1545 for £498; he also gave land in Pitchcroft to the Worcester Corporation, on condition that they erected a Free School in the City in order:

*'to bring up youthes
in their a.b.c., mattens,
evensong, and other lernynge.'*

Thomas Wylde was was a Member of Parliament for Worcester (1701 to 1727).

EDWARD ELGAR

# Chapter five

# Interesting people of Worcester, some famous, some not so famous

**Amos, Alan**

It was Alan Amos (a Labour Councillor in a Tory-run Council, led by Simon Geraghty), who first suggested that Worcester should become the first British city to be twinned with Gaza City. He was quoted as saying (in the Daily Mail):

*'Like many I have watched the plight of the people of Gaza, seeing them get bombed and bombed by Israelis with advanced military weapons. But rather than sit there thinking, "Isn't that terrible" I really wanted to do something about it.*

*We wanted to bring people together to show a gesture of solidarity – so Gaza could look at us and see that the whole world isn't against them, there are people who understand their plight and think what is happening to them is unacceptable. We are optimistic this will go ahead. And it is a humanitarian gesture and not a political move.'*

**Allen, Sir Roy George Douglas,** CBE, FBA

Sir Roy George Douglas Allen (1906–1983) was born in Worcester and educated at the Royal Grammar School Worcester. He became a lecturer at the London School of Economics, and later he became a Professor of Statistics. He wrote papers on the following:

A Reconsideration of the Theory of Value (1934)
Mathematical Analysis for Economists (1938)
Statistics for Economists (1949)
Mathematical Economics (1956)
Macroeconomic Theory (1967)

**Atkinson, The Very Revd. Peter**

One thousand people attended Worcester Cathedral when the Very Revd. Peter Atkinson (aged 54) was installed as the 46th Dean of Worcester (April 28, 2007). The service was conducted by the Bishop of Worcester, the Rt. Rev. Peter Selby. Very Revd. Peter Atkinson is the current Dean and lives at The Deanery, College Green, Worcester.

**Baldwin, Sir Stanley**

Stanley Baldwin, 1st Earl Baldwin of Bewdley, kg, pc (1867–1947), was a conservative politician, statesman, and served three terms as Prime Minister. He was born at Lower Park House, Bewdley.

On his mother's side, Louisa, Sir Stanley was a first cousin of the writer and poet, Rudyard Kipling. After a long active career, Sir Stanley Baldwin was created the Earl Baldwin of Bewdley after the coronation of King George VI. He resigned the next day and was created a Knight of the Garter. His ashes are buried in Worcester cathedral and is commemorated by a square stone slab.

### Barnes, Samuel

Some 250 years ago, a certain Samuel Barnes, baker and malster in Newport Street, had installed for himself a newly invented machine, the best of its kind, for making oatmeal; it was said to be most efficient and very reasonably priced.

### Bennett, Robert

Bennetts Farms is Worcester's very own family-run, dairy farm and manufacturer of fine ice cream and sorbet. The business was started by Robert Bennett (right), who was born the eldest of eight children, near Saint Ives Cornwall in 1870. He left the family smallholding to support himself as soon as he was able. He left home and ventured into the dairy business in the South East of England. Several years later he was running his own dairy in White Hart Lane, Tottenham.

In 1918 Robert Bennett finally moved back out into the country, buying Manor Farm in Worcestershire which is situated in the river meadows of the Severn valley. Robert, together with his son Stanley, built up a substantial dairy herd.

His son Stanley (T S Bennett) also found the time to enter local politics and during his period in office as Mayor of Worcester he was able to grant the Freedom of the city to Winston Churchill – a deed of admission, which was contained in an ebony plinth of a specially designed jardiniere, which was created at the Royal Porcelain Works.

In 1965 Stanley's son, John, took over the business and built it up further. During this time he started the ice cream manufacturing which has now been in operation for over 30 years.

Today two of Robert Bennett's great grandsons, Keith and Duncan, run the ice cream business whilst another great grandson, Christopher manages the farm and in particular the dairy herd of over 200 Holstein and Fresian cows. This herd is at the 250-acre Manor Farm which lies along 3 miles of the river. The famous ice cream is sold locally and also in the South and East of the country.

## Berkeley, Robert George Wilmot

Robert George Wilmot Berkeley (1898–1969), who lived at Berkley Castle and Spetchley Park, was High Sheriff of Worcestershire in 1933, and Deputy Lieutenant of the county in 1952.

Robert Berkley played four times in first-class cricket for Worcestershire County Cricket Club.

## Bonaparte, Lucien

Lucien Bonaparte (1775–1840), younger brother of Napoleon, lived for a few years at Grimley, just outside Worcester having been captured by the British at sea whilst trying to escape into exile to America, following breakdown of relations with his brother, the Emperor Napoleon.

The British Government had permitted Lucien Bonaparte to buy Thorngrove, where his son Louis-Lucien was born in 1813, while he was working on a heroic poem, on the subject of Charlemagne.

Napoleon, believing Lucien had deliberately gone to Britain and thus a traitor, had Lucien omitted from the Imperial almanacs of the Bonapartes from 1811 onward.

## Bonham, Reginald Walter

Reginald Bonham (1906–1984), like others in his family, was born visually impaired. Aged 16, he was sent to the Worcester College for the Blind, where he revealed a talent for playing chess. While attending Saint Catherine's College Oxford in 1929, Reginald won the Oxford Chess Championship.

Reginald Bonham returned to Worcester College for the Blind, as a teacher. Known as 'Bon' by the staff, he taught many subjects, such as maths, braille, drama, bridge and chess.

Bonham won numerous chess tournaments, and in 1934, he founded the Braille Chess Magazine, which he wrote and edited for 25 years.

## Bray, Sir Reginald

Sir Reginald Bray (1440–1503), second son of Sir Richard Bray, was born in Worcester. He was created Knight of the Bath at the coronation of Henry VII. He was also Treasurer, restructuring the King's finances. As an architect he designed the following buildings:

Henry VII's Chapel at Westminster.
Saint Georges's Chapel in Windsor Castle.
Great Malvern Priory.

### Brock, Sir Thomas

Sir Thomas Brock KCB RA (1847–1922), was born in Worcester. He undertook an apprenticeship in modelling at the Worcester Royal Porcelain Works.

In 1866 he was a pupil of the sculptor John Henry Foley, collaborating with Foley and later became a very famous sculptor in his own right, attributed to the many fine works, including:

Statue of Prince Albert for Albert Memorial, London.
Equestrian statue of the Black Prince for the City Square, Leeds.
'The Moment of Peril' and 'Eve' at the Tate Gallery, London.
Sir Richard Owen.
Statue of Henry Philpott, Bishop of Worcester.
Bust of Lord Leighton in Saint Paul's Cathedral, London.
Statue of John Everett Millais, painter, Tate Gallery, London.
Longfellow bust for poets Corner in Westminster Abbey.
Statue of Edward VII, New Delhi.
Richard Baxter memorial at Kidderminster.
Imperial Memorial to Queen Victoria, Buckingham Palace.

*Statue of Queen Victoria, Carlton House Terrace, London*

### Bryan, Stephen

Stephen Bryan (1690–1748) lived on the south side of the Cross Keys, Sidbury. He was a proprietor, printer and publisher of the Worcester Postman from 1709 for forty years. He sold the Worcester Postman to Harry Berrow. John Tymbs, married Berrow's daughter, later became proprietor of the Worcester Postman and wrote of Stephen Bryan:

> If we may judge him by his paper, he was a modest, quite a little fellow, honest, outspoken and plain of speech, and yet carrying an unconscious assumption of knowledge in his manner.'

### Bullingham, Nicholas

Nicholas Bullingham (1520–1576) was born in Worcester. He attended the Royal Grammar School. Completing his education, he entered the church, and became private chaplain to Elizabeth I. He became Bishop of Worcester in 1574.

### Burkill, Peter – A hero from Worcester

A report by the Air Accidents Investigation Branch (September, 2008) ruled that it was ice in the fuel system of the Boeing 777, that caused the engines to fail, and for it to crash-land at Heathrow in January 2008. Lauren Rogers of Worcester News (September, 2008) reported the following:

> 'Captain Peter Burkill, who lived at King Stephen's Mount, Saint John's, Worcester, was the pilot of the Boeing 777. His quick-thinking action to counter the angle of the

*plane's wing flaps helped his co-pilot John Coward to successfully land the aircraft. The plane came to a stop on grass and 136 passengers plus the 16 crew escaped without serious injury.'*

## Burrows, Herbert

*A constable's fatal slip*

It was early on a cold winter's morning in 1925, when 22-year-old police constable, Herbert Burrows, rushed up to a colleague on point duty at The Cross, telling him that an innkeeper, his wife and child, had been murdered in the early hours, at the Garibaldi pub in Wyld's Lane.

The problem for Constable Herbert Burrows, was, that the brutal murder hadn't been reported or even discovered at the time. Colleague P.C.Devey asked how he knew of the crime. Burrows replied that a man in Lowesmoor had told him. But this conversation sealed Burrows own death warrant.

It appears that Burrows was the last person left drinking at the Garibaldi. The following morning the pub charlady arrived and together with a neighbour contacted the police, who on arrival were confronted with a terrible scene. The body of 31-year-old licensee, Ernest George Laight, together with his 30-year-old wife Doris, was lying on the cellar floor. Both had died from bullet wounds.

Upstairs their two-year-old son Robert was dead in his cot, having died from a fractured skull, but his six-year-old sister was discovered still alive.

Having given himself away, detectives went to Burrow's home, in Wyld's Lane. There they discovered a revolver and ammunition. On Examination of the said revolver, it was found to be the same gun that had killed the Laight family. In a suitcase they found £65. When searching Burrows, they found a further £22. Burrows made a full confession.

The motive for the crime was, that Burrows had been in debt to money-lenders. He also wanted cash for a holiday, due to begin the following day.

*Constable Herbert Burrows' written statement reads:*

*'I voluntarily and fully admit that I killed, at 12.50 am, on November 27, 1925, Mr and Mrs Laight and Robert Laight.*

*I apologise to the officers and men of the Worcester City Police for the disgrace thus incurred'*

Burrows was the last Worcester murderer to go to the gallows. He was hanged at Gloucester Jail on February 17, 1926, by Albert Pierrepoint.

## Burrowes, Thomas

Thomas Burrowes (1796–1866) was born in Worcester. He served as a Corporal in the Royal Sappers and Miners, which provided military engineering and other technical support to the British Armed Forces, from 1813 until 1824. He was posted to Fort

Henry in Kingston, Upper Canada, in 1815. Burrowes served as the Assistant overseer of Works for the Rideau Canal project in Ontario, Canada. He is mainly known for his series of watercolour paintings documenting the construction of this important project.

He worked and lived in Ontario, becoming Clerk of the Works of the Cataraqui section of the Rideau Canal until retirement.

In retirement, Burrowes worked as a farmer, supplementing his income by serving both as a postmaster and Justice of the Peace in Kingston Mills. Burrowes died in 1866 at his home,

*Lower Bytown, now the city of Ottawa, from the Barrack Hill, near the head of the Eighth Lock and the 'Sappers' Bridge', 1845*

Maplehurst, overlooking the Rideau waterway and Kingston, the cottage still stands today. Burrowes' paintings have been referred to as some of the most famous and valuable images in Ontario history.

## Butler, Samuel

Samuel Butler (1612–1680), poet and satirist, was the son of a farmer in Strensham, and educated at the King's School in Worcester. He wrote 'Hudibras' which was published in three parts in 1663, 1664 and 1678, it is a satire on the Cromwellians and on the Presbyterian church written by a confirmed Royalist and Anglican. Hudibras, a colonel in the Cromwellian army, is involved in various comic misadventures and is shown to be stupid, greedy and dishonest. The poem is very well written in Chaucerian couplets and was popular for about 150 years, as long as its political attitudes were also popular. It was understood that King Charles II admired this work and promised Samuel Butler a generous pension. Samuel Butler is buried in Westminster Abbey.

## Cam, W H

During Victorian times John Cam (father of John James Cam) had workshops at 32 The Shambles, where, for 50 years, he produced sewing machines, knives and presses. His son, John, joined him before becoming an inventor and industrialist and developing the Cam Engineering Works in Charles Street.

## John James Cam

John James Cam (1850 –1919) one of eight children, he joined his father's company in the Shambles in the early 1870s and developed into an inventor and engineer. joined his father's company, W. H. Cam at the Excelsior Works at 32 The Shambles. John James became an amazing engineer and inventor. He repaired motor cars and motorcycles, made machinery for the clothing industry, built motorcycles, produced a one and a half horse power tandem, and established a revered name in the motoring history pioneering many key components: the carburettor, the radiator, handlebar controls and braking systems for motor cycles. He also built the engines for the organ of Worcester's Public Hall as well as the Cathedral and was founder member of the Worcestershire Camera Club and Worcester Tricycle Club.

A 'Blue Plaque' can be seen on the wall of 4 Charles Street which was the site of his purpose-built works.

## Chambers, John

John Chambers was a London architect who settled in Worcester in 1810. He spent eight years researching the history of the area. His book 'History of Worcester' was published in 1817.

## Chamberlain, Robert

Robert Chamberlain (1736–1798), was born in Worcester. He was one of the famous Worcester porcelain decorators and painters. He started his own porcelain works at Diglis. When he died, his two sons, (partners in the business Chamberlain & Co.) allowed the company to expand, and it was given a Royal Warrant in 1807.

## Chettell, Richard

Richard Chettell met a violent death in 1645, during the occupation of the Royalists in the City.

There is a monument dedicated to him in All Saints Church which states:

*'of the massacred gent: Mr Richard Chettell, deceased, 19 March, 1645.'*

His grandson, Thomas Chettell, was twice High Bailiff. Thomas, a very kindly soul, distributed fifty petticoats to the poor of All Saints parish, so that they could at least keep warm in the cold winter months.

## Chicken George

This much-loved Worcester character was so well-known that artists even included him in their paintings, in an effort to capture the city street-life. His real name was George Webb. He was a very patriotic man, claiming to have served in the Worcestershire regiment. He also claimed to have fought in the war at Dunkirk and during the fighting had killed one of the enemy. In fact he stated:

*'I got a bayonet wound in me 'head from Dunkirk – but I got him, I lived and he didn't…'*

His erratic dancing resembled that of a pecking chicken. George was often seen dancing to the music of street buskers, much to the amusement of those passing by. Some buskers didn't like his particular quirky dancing, his sense of humour, his devilish mood, and his profanities. But nevertheless George did have a strong bond with buskers.

George Webb always attended the Remembrance Day Parades, and never failed to attend Worcestershire regimental reunions. In later years he had lived in Lowesmoor, but poor health meant that a stay in hospital was inevitable. Unable to look after himself, he spent the last weeks of his life at Saint Cloud's Nursing Home, in Callow End. He died in 2006, at the age of 86.

Sue Jones who was the manageress of Saint Cloud's at the time, said that George's character in those last days of his life, still remained as vibrant as ever. She is quoted as saying:

*'He never lost his sense of humour. It stayed with him to the end.*
*He was a very popular character.*
*All the girls knew who he was and he was totally charming.'*

## Clapton, Nathaniel Langford

Nathaniel Langford Clapton (1903–1967), was born in Worcester. He was the only son of Nathaniel Clapton, an ironmonger's manager, of Saint Dunstan's Crescent. Nathaniel attended the Royal Grammar School, Worcester, and gained first class honours in Mathematical Moderations in 1923, at Hertford College, Oxford.

Nathaniel Clapton was Senior Mathematics Master at Watford Grammar School and The Glasgow Academy. He was headmaster of Boteler Grammar School, Warrington for ten years, and was Headmaster at King Edward VII School, Sheffield, in 1950 for a further 15 years.

## Clapton, Nicholas

Nicholas Clapton (1955–), an opera singer, was born in Worcester and read music at Magdalen College, Oxford. He made his professional debut at Wigmore Hall in 1984. In 1985 he was a double prize-winner at the Concurso 'Francisco Viñas' in Barcelona, and in 1987 he won the English Song Award.

Nicholas is particularly known for counter-tenor roles in contemporary opera; and has performed in major opera houses and concert halls around the world, having given twenty-seven world premières.

## Clifford, Bonnie

Bonnie's father, Brian Keogh (1926–2006), was an accountant for Lea & Perrins for many years, and he retired from the company in 1991. He died at the age of 80. Bonnie was working with the Worcester Museum, having discovered some of her father's valuable documents which were connected with Lea & Perrins.

Bonnie Clifford lives not far from me in Perdiswell Street; and I had arranged that Bonnie and her sister, Isabel, meet up over a cup of tea. That was when Bonnie related to me the following:

IN 1837 MESSRS. LEA & PERRINS STARTED MANUFACTURING WORCESTERSHIRE SAUCE AT THEIR PREMISES IN BROAD STREET WORCESTER. IT IS STILL APPRECIATED THROUGHOUT THE WORLD TODAY

*'Mum (Mary Timbers) and Dad (Brian Keogh) met in Paris in 1947, which was the first year when people were free to travel again after the war. Dad, who came from Glasgow, had joined the Argyll & Sutherland Highlanders as soon as he left school at 18, and saw some service in Germany. Dad was officially, the youngest soldier at the Rhine Crossing.*

*He was, he said, not as afraid of the Germans as he was of the mortar bombs which he had to carry.*

*Mum, who was born in Worcester, was a teacher who had trained at Whitelands College in London during the war, and, after teaching in Dover for one year, had returned to Worcester.'*

*It was just after the war ended (August, 1945), when people could once again go abroad for their holidays, that my mother decided to go to Paris for the weekend with a friend, that's when she first met dad. Dad was also on holiday in Paris for a few days, with a mate of his. It was quite accidental that both parties should sit alongside each other on a coach trip to the Eifel Tower. The four of them started chatting, and got quite friendly.*

*On the return coach journey, dad arranged to meet mum the next day; and when they parted at the coach station, there was dad shouting out: "Don't forget! Two o'clock tomorrow!" And so it was that they fell in love. Dad went back home to Glasgow, Mum going home to 16 Summer Street in Barbourne, where she was born and brought up.*

*In 1948, Mum and Dad got married at Saint Stephen's Church. They had three daughters: Isabel, Janet and myself. Mum taught at Nunnery Wood Primary School, in Prestwich Avenue, and we three sisters went there, moving on to the Girls Grammar School, where some of the teachers had also taught our Mum!*

*'Isabel and Janet decided to become nurses, while I went on a teacher's training course, and became a teacher in Hampshire.*

*I came back to Worcester in 1989, with my son James and daughter Katherine, and two cats called Thunder and Tiger and bought a house in Perdiswell Street a few doors down from my sister Isabel. Being so close has been quite a blessing to us both ever since. The children have stayed the same but the cats are different!*

*At the moment I am working with Worcester Museum to sort out all the artifacts and papers we have relating to Lea & Perrins and the final resting place of the original recipe book, which Dad found in a skip. This fits in well with the passion I have for archaeology and local history.'*

## Cocks, Lady Margaret

Margaret, Countess of Hardwicke (sister to Lady Williams) was the daughter of Charles Cocks MP of Worcester and Mary Somers. Margaret was a niece of Lord Chancellor Somers. She married Philip Yorke, 1st Earl of Hardwicke in 1719. Together they had seven children:

Philip Yorke, 2nd Earl of Hardwicke (1720–1790)
Hon. Charles Yorke (1722–1770)
General Sir Joseph Yorke (Lord Dover) (1723–92)
Lady Elizabeth Yorke (1725–1760)
Hon John Yorke (1728–1801)
Rt. Rev. James Yorke, Bishop of Ely (1730–1808)
Lady Margaret Yorke (1733–1769)

Lady Margaret did a lot of charitable work in Worcester; her date of her birth is unknown; she died, at a great loss to all in 1761.

## Cook, Edgar Thomas

Edgar Thomas Cook c.b.e. d.mus. f.r.c.o. f.r.c.m. (1880–1953), organist and composer, was born in Worcester and sent to Royal Grammar School. He began his career as a church organist in 1898. Six years later he was assistant organist at Worcester Cathedral under Sir Ivor Atkins, and he attained an Organ Scholarship to Queens College, Oxford.

Edgar Thomas Cook became organist at Southwark Cathedral, where he remained for the rest of his life. He became famous for his lunch-time concerts on BBC during the 1930s and 1940s.

## Corbett, Edward C

Edward C. Corbett (1870–1952) followed in his father's footsteps, became a solicitor in Worcester. He was quite a character and purely by chance, while on holiday in London, he ended up at the London Docks. There he was asked by a ship's officer if he was looking for a berth; the next moment he was sailing to Australia, where he spent several years.

Edward Corbett returned to England in 1914, and at 43 years, being too old to be called-up, became a volunteer in the Battalion (Territorial Force) of the Worcestershire Regiment, where he rose to the rank of sergeant, and was awarded the Military Medal for bravery at the Battle of the Somme. With WWI over, Edward Corbett found it difficult finding a job. Eventually, in 1922, he found work with Lea & Perrins, working as a labourer.

When the senior office staff discovered that Edward was able to speak many languages, they offered the job of a sales rep. in the export trade. Thus in 1924, he began to travel for the firm to Australia, New Zealand; then later travelling to Brazil and the Argentine.

I have included two letters. The first one is just n part of a letter from Edward Corbett in Barbados to Lea & Perrins Ltd. in Worcester:

*Ocean View Hotel, Hastings (near Bridgetown), Barbados*
*3rd December, 1934*
*To: Lea & Perrins Ltd, Worcester*

*Dear Sirs,*

*Since my last detailed letter I have visited British and Dutch Guyana, completed work in Trinidad, and come here to Barbados, from which I propose to sail tomorrow in the Canadian mailboat 'Lady Hawkins' to the Antillas. She calls at them all for a few hours as far as Saint Kitts, where I must stay three days, returning by the sister ship 'Lady Nelson,' which touches at all on the way back. By this means, If I miss a customer on the trip North, I stand to catch him on the way South again.*
*I also get a reduced fare for the return trip by the same Line.*

*I am due back here on the 13th, and at Trinidad – after touching at Granada and Saint Vincent – on the 15th. On that day the Royal Netherlands Liner 'Crijnssen' will be able to take me to Curazao and Panama.*

*It seems that I must leave out Venezuela, a very vexing thing, as we have in that country a number of good customers who have not bought so much the last year or two; also a very good agent in Leopold Quintero at Caracas.*

*But I am advised that the Venezolan Government, which has always made landing difficult for foreigners, really does not want them now, and since the recent political murders in Europe have proved the futility of the passport system, has issued new regulations of such stringency as I cannot comply with without waiting hereabouts for an unconscionable time. Passengers from Trinidad are particularly suspect, as that is the usual refuge for Venezolan exiles.*

*The last ships from that Coast report that passengers are not allowed to visit Caracas from La Guayra....*

The second letter reads:

*Anglo-American Hotel, Managua, Nicaragua, Barbados*
*3rd February, 1936*
*To: Lea & Perrins Ltd, Worcester*

*Dear Sirs,*

*I landed at Corinto on the 24th January, too late for that day's train up country, and saw our only customer there, Mr Griffiths, the Vice-consul, who now imports for up-country clients, chiefly at Leon and in the mining district of Ocotal (Nueva Segovia), where there is considerable development at present. From him I was able to get Cordobas (the local currency) at a fair price for my sterling, thus saving 30 per cent from the price officially fixed by the Board of Control for dealings in Banks.*

*As in Costa Rica this Control is paralysing trade. Officially it is very strict, permission has to be sought to import even necessaries, among which our brand is reckoned.*

*In practice this permission is never refused, but notice is given that drafts for payment will not be available before next September, so only those who have credits abroad are able to import, unless they have some other means of getting foreign moneys.*

*Even exporters must surrender their drafts; species and money must not be exported, and travellers are not allowed to take with them more than 200 dollars. I have been lucky in getting 97.50 dollars for £20 from a merchant of Managua who wanted sterling.*

*In these circumstances it may be imagined that I had no chance of placing any orders for H.P. products. It is true that a good many customers, finding stocks low, ordered L. & P. and have little doubt of receiving permission to import it; but all agreed that there was no chance of introducing new lines. Except Mr Ballantyne, manager of P. J. Frawley at Leon.*

*He is going to try; it is vinegar that he chiefly wants; and he is so important in the country, and stands so well with Government on account of his work in promoting the gold-mining industry, that he may very well succeed.*

*Please observe the yellow card relating to this firm. If an agent for H.P. is to be appointed here, I recommend it. The best of agents would not be very successful just now, but the general opinion of the best judges is that by the end of the year the Control will be ended or at least greatly relaxed, and business resumed on normal lines.*

*This opinion is based on the great increase in the output of gold. If it be well founded, the appointment of a good agent in the next few months would give the lines a good chance; for on the release of commerce there would follow great enterprise in ordering. The merchant houses at least are far from short of money.*

## Conditions

*Since the decisive victory of the Liberals or national party, whose centre was Leon, and the departure of the North American forces the country has gone ahead in a wonderful way, and improvements are visible on all sides.*

*The Government is without doubt very capable, and employs capable men of either party. The victors have behaved with surprising generosity to the Conservatives, especially considering the shameful treatment received from them, and I found our Granadan customers doing well, although their town was the focus of the Conservatives.*

*So the country is not only at peace but content and full of hope. A little too cocksure perhaps, but it is a pleasure to find a people not in a bog of depression.*

*The end of the guerrilla in the North has reopened that great tract of valuable country, and minerals, timber and coffee are coming in again from there.*

## Stocks

*I found stocks very low, as Houses are not allowed to import much at a time, and as the demand is good these small parcels do not last long.*

*Most of the orders given at my calls were for four or five cases; only two asked for as many as ten, but the two both stand well and I hope will gain the necessary leave. In fact I think more orders will pass on from here than from Costa Rica, where stocks are equally low and inability to supply will (I fear) affect the demand.*

## Communications

*These are greatly improved since the wars, especially the railways, but carriage is still costly and adds a good deal to the cost of our brand, already handicapped by heavy duties, and still more by the exchange.*

## Managua

*The capital is being slowly rebuilt after the earthquake, and as it has to be done with local moneys it is being done modestly and sensibly and with good effect.*

*But earthquake, fire and looting ruined several of our customers, and I found the personnel much changed. The survivors are, it is true, more solid than most of the former importers. Don Benito Ramirez is chief of them.*

## Leon

*The ancient City is recovered from its troubles, and thanks to improved roads and a branch railway has regained the trade of the North-west of which the Conservatives and Yanquis robbed it in the day of their power. But the troubles fell heavily on the chiefs of the place, and of all our old customers only two are left. But these are very solid-Robelo and Frawley- and two solid importers are enough for a place of the size.*

*Griffiths of Corinto imports for some of the shops, and the few grocers and numerous druggists all seem to sell the brand. They could sell more if they could get it.*

*The country round about is very well tilled, in striking contrast to the districts of Managua and Granada, and there is plenty of money in the place.*

## Granada

*The trade of the Great Lake keeps the town flourishing and as the Liberals did not avenge upon Granada the treatment of Leon, most of the old firms are still there. But few of them are now able to import, and Guarrero Castillo has most of the business to our great pain, for he is as solid as a rock. Eitzen & Arnold are a good house, but I do not think so much of the Sons of Agustin Chamorro.*

## Masaya

*There is fairly good farming round here, and a good trade of supplying the Southern coffee district. Moreover the volcano which destroyed so much coffee has ceased to smoke.*

*But nearly all the grocery business is in the hands of Castillo, and the only other importer is Quant, a very sound man. I did not go to Rivas, as there was a gale on the Lake and the boat was not running. None of the other country towns are in a position under the Control to repay the time and expense of a visit.*

*I leave here on the 5th by plane for Honduras, Salvador and Guatemala. The fare is only 46 dollars, and I may stop off for as long as I like at Tegucigalpa and San Salvador. It is much cheaper than travel by ship, and for some reason passengers by air are excused all those troubles of questionnaires and deposits that make arrival by ship in Central America such a scourge and delay to the traveller.*

*One does not care to deposit £100 for the privilege of a week's visit to such absurd little countries. And it is not easy to get it back on leaving*

*Yours obediently*

*Edward C Corbett*

## Crazy Buffalo (Stephen Ballard)

Crazy Buffalo (1940–2008), of Thorn Avenue, Brickfields, was an honorary member of the North American Blackfoot tribe in the 1970s. He changed his name by deed poll in 1992, and set up a group called the Crown East Indians; regularly attending local schools and talking to the children about Red Indian culture.

Crazy Buffalo was best known for his handmade Red Indian outfits, including his feathered headdress. And, for his rain dance in 1995; when six days later the rains came, alienating a serious drought in the area.

Sadly, in 1996, his son David was killed in a road accident in Worcester, whilst walking home from a friend's funeral. It was in 2006, when Crazy Buffalo was diagnosed with cancer of the oesophagus, which spread to his bowel. He died two years later. A feathered headdress was placed on is coffin, at the cremation on Christmas Eve, 2008.

## Private Frederick George Dancox V.C.

Private Frederick Dancox, of the 4th Battalion Worcestershire Regiment, was the city's only born and bred winner of the Victoria Cross, Britain's highest honour for gallantry under fire, gained during the First World War on 9 October 1917 at the Battle of Poelcappelle, Ypres, 9th October 1917. He was 38 years old. He was given leave to return to England and receive the medal from King George V, but his leave was cancelled in the wake of a German counter-

*The memorial plaque to George Dancox, designed by Sam Eedle from Tewkesbury, at the Deansway entrance to Crowngate Shopping Centre*

attack near Masnieres, France, in the Battle of Cambrai, on 30 November 1917, and he was killed in action. His body was never found.

A memorial plaque to George Dancox, designed by Sam Eedle from Tewkesbury, was unveiled in Crowngate Shopping Centre in 2010. It is similar to a memorial near to the village of Langemarck in Belgium, close to the site, where Private Dancox single-handed, captured an enemy block-house; taking German gunners prisoner.

## Dent, Thomas – The Glove Maker

Thomas Dent was apprenticed for seven years in the glovemaking business with his father John Dent Senior, at 26 Sidbury. The firm, founded in 1777, then became known as John Dent & Sons.

Thomas Dent's father drowned in the River Severn in 1811. Thomas's elder brother John had established a glove manufacturing business several years before his father's death; and a younger brother, William had joined him; thus the firm became known as J & W Dent & Co. and these three brothers became very prominent in the glove making industry.

It was while I was watching the Antique Roadshow in September, 2008, that I discovered that John and William Dent had bought Sudeley Castle and estate (which was once the home of Catherine Parr; and Lady Jane Grey) in 1837. John and William Dent began its restoration, and today the castle stands as a wonderful monument to the restorers, and boasts of beautiful apartments with tapestries and paintings by Rubens, Turner and Van Dyck. It is the home of Lord and Lady Ashcombe and the Dent-Brocklehurst family.

After the tax was lifted on foreign gloves in 1826, French gloves became popular, causing a decline in the glove manufacture in this country; leading to mass unemployment. Dent, Allcroft and Company managed to survive by reorganising their workforce and improving overall quality; and became a leading glove manufacturer in Europe.

In 1898, Dent, Allcroft and Company were at 96 Wood Street; later they moved to Warmstry House by the River Severn, which was formerly occupied by Flight & Barr Porcelain Company. The glove factory was demolished in 1970, in order to make way for the Worcester Technical College Buildings.

## Dhonau, Mary

Mary Dhonau who campaigned for flood victims, received an OBE in the Queen's Birthday Honours List of 2009. Mary, while living in Diglis, became a flood victim herself in the year 2000. Mary took a key role in getting flood defences up in Hylton Road; she also played an important role in the residents' campaign group for 'Worcester Action Against Flooding.

## Dingle, Francis

Francis Dingle (1829–1915) was Mayor of Worcester in 1877. He owned the King Charles Pub in the Cornmarket, also a large licensed premises at the corner of Broad Street and Angel Place. Dingle also bought 11 houses in Butts Walk, three houses in Infirmary Walk, four houses in London Road and Portefields Villa, near Shrub Hill Station.

Francis Dingle lived with his wife Georgina Maria Dingle, at Thames House, in Barbourne, opposite Saint George's Square, where Worcester Grammar School for Girls was built in the 1920s. In this house they brought up their ten children.

## Duncan, John

In 1819, John Duncan and his family emigrated to New York, where he opened a grocery shop in the Broadway; it's on record that he first imported Lea & Perrins Worcestershire Sauce in 1840. His son David, became a partner, which was then called John Duncan & Son.

In 1850, his second son, John Patterson, also became a partner. In 1853, John Duncan became sole agent for the United States. At that time the family had moved from their small premises at 407 Broadway, to their grand new five-storey building next door. The businesses on both sides of the Atlantic expanded; but by the time the American Civil War came to an end in 1865, John Duncan, the founder of the company had died.

## Edwards, Patricia

I met Patricia Jill Edwards and her husband Charles, as my neighbours in Barbourne. For the last 33 years, Jill (as she likes to be called), has been a school crossing supervisor or a 'Lollipop' lady for the Northwick Junior and Infant School, which is in Northwick Road, Worcester (the School Crossing Patrol Service was introduced in this country in the 1950s).

Jill's father, Charles Ramsey, was born in Tallow Hill. He worked at a tanning factory which was by the canal in Worcester, till it closed down. Charles then went to work for Ebenezer Baylis & Son Limited, printers in London Road, Worcester; he retired from there in 1912.

Patricia's mother was Helen Band.

Jill remembered:

*'I was born at 10 Rowan Avenue. There were twelve of us living there, including three of my uncles (Ray, Mike, and Alfred), in a three-bedroomed house. Mum was both a housewife and part-time cleaner at Lloyd's Bank in the city. My grandmother died when mum was only 22 years old. So my mum had to look after her brothers and sisters. Altogether there were seven of them, living with us at Rowan Avenue; the youngest being*

*only six months old when his mum died. Mum had it down to a fine art, looking after the twelve of us in this three-bedroom house. The men slept in one room; women in the other, auntie Rene, her husband and their two boys in another bedroom.*

*'Mum got married at Saint Peter's in 1951. She had three daughters: the eldest was Audrey; then there was Pam; I was the youngest. I had two twin brothers that died in mother's womb. Mum was supreme ruler; when she said 'do this' or 'don't do that', you obeyed – you never crossed mum. She wasn't spiteful; she never ever laid a hand to us; the tone of her voice, was enough to make all of us obedient. My sisters and I had house chores to do; even when I was courting Charlie, for those five years, I had to finish my chores before I could go out with him.*

*We all went to Gorse Hill School. I still remember two of my teachers: Mr Green; and Mr Cooley. I left school at the age of 14. I worked in a toy and wool shop at Albion House in Broad Street. I went to work at the International Stores in the Cross in 1965. I got the sack from there, because I was suffering from achalasia (meaning 'failure to relax'). It's a rare disease of the muscle of the esophagus, and I had great difficulty in swallowing. I was getting chest pains and having breathing problems. I was not allowed to lie flat, I had to be propped up, using a 'v' pillow. I was quite ill for several years, during which time I lost six stone in weight, and ending up having a surgical operation. My son Nick was seven when I started working again as a school crossing supervisor.'*

## Elgar, Sir Edward

Edward Elgar (1857–1934) was born, the fourth of their seven children, in a small red-brick cottage on the road leading to Broadheath. When Edward was two years old, the family moved into Worcester, where they lived above his father's music shop in the High Street. The very young Elgar coached a little by his father, and self-taught in music, began piano and violin lessons at the age of seven. He attained experience with local performing chamber groups and orchestras and by the age of sixteen was a  proficient enough musician to support himself as a freelance violinist and teacher. His father, William Henry Elgar, was a piano tuner, an organist at the Catholic church for 35 years, and a violinist playing in the 'Three Choirs Festival Orchestra.' In 1884, Edward took over from his father as organist. He was also a music teacher at a girls' school in Malvern, and gave private tuition. But, his ambition was to be a composer.

Edward was 32, when he married Alice Roberts, an ex-pupil and the daughter of a major-general who was against the marriage and disowned his daughter marrying this unknown Catholic musician. She was his business manager and social secretary, dedicating her life to him, and his music, until her death.

In 1897 Elgar's work was recognised in Germany, and in 1899 as a composer in this country. He wrote some of the world's most moving, delicate and profound works. His output ranged from the sweet gentleness of 'Salut D'amour' to the spiritual

grandeur of his oratorio, 'The Dream of Gerontius;' also 'Enigma Variations,' and 'Pomp and Circumstance' marches.

Elgar is regarded as the Shakespeare of music; he injected an unmistakable Englishness into everything he wrote. More than any other British composer, he showed the sensitive side of the English soul in his music.

For years he was out of fashion. His work was dismissed as little more than flag-waving band music. 'Pomp and Circumstance No.1, part of which became the anthem Land of Hope and Glory, was seized on by his detractors as little more than linguistic nonsense – an argument reinforced by its use at every Last Night of the Proms. Elgar was just merely reciting the flashy spirit of Edwardian Britain. Land of Hope and Glory, for instance, was used as part of the Coronation Ode for King Edward VII.

Elgar's. sacred music has proved to be his most profound work. His brilliance is all the more amazing when you consider that he was self-taught.

*At the end of the High Street stands the bronze statue of Sir Edward Elgar by Kenneth Potts, a designer at the Royal Worcester Porcelain Works at the time, in 1979. The statue unveiled by the Prince of Wales on 2 June 1981, with a celebratory concert of Elgar's music held in Worcester Cathedral afterwards.*

Edward Elgar was frequently short of cash, his wife had to draw manuscript paper by hand for him as they couldn't afford to by any, and Elgar was often forced to do to teaching.

It was not until 1899, at the age of 42, that he received huge acclaim with the 'Variations'. Elgar became a national celebrity; his music ringing from concert halls. Much to the embarrassment of his snooty critics, Elgar also became a friend of royalty. King George V and Queen Mary liked his music.

After his wife's death in 1920, Sir Edward Elgar moved back to Kempsey, near Worcester, to live.

In 1931 Sir Edward Elgar was made a baron, added to his other awards: 1904, Knight Bachelor; 1911, Order of Merit; 1928, Knight Commander of the Royal Victorian Order; and in 1933, Elgar was promoted within the Royal Victorian Order to Knight Grand Cross. He was now 'Sir Edward Elgar Bt OM GCVO' and received the highly prestigious Order of Merit.

One of his greatest passions was his much-adored Malvern Hills, and with his music, Elgar captures the English countryside perfectly.

The 150th anniversary of Sir Edward Elgar's birth in 2007, didn't stop the Bank of England from removing his image from the back of our £20 notes.

## Forster, Sir Charles,

Sir Charles Forster, 1st Baronet (1815–1891), son of Charles Smith Forster, was born in Worcester and became a Liberal politician, representing Walsall in the 19th century.

## Gavron, `Felicia Nicolette 'Nicky'

Felicia Nicolette Gavron, the daughter of a German Jew who had fled Nazi Germany in 1936, was born in Worcester (1945). Nicky studied at Worcester Girls' Grammar School, and later at the history of art at the Courtauld Institute in London. She became a politician, former Deputy Mayor of London under Ken Livingstone, and also a member of the London Assembly.

## Glazzard, Mrs K

Mrs Glazzard relates the following story

*'I have spent most of my life in Worcester. I am married and have raised up four sons, twins. They all have different personalities. But this story is mainly about one of the twins.*

*'At the age of 14, one of my twin sons decided to do survival as a hobby, so I helped him by getting books from the library for him to look at. His brother Phil, however, enjoyed watching magic shows and got interested in the art of illusions. So, for the twin's birthday I bought a survival package for one and for Phil I bought a box of magic tricks, from which he learned to do slight of hand tricks, and over a period of time got quite proficient.*

*'When Phil left school, and went into employment, he bought more magic tricks to widen his performance. Then, together with his girlfriend (who became his assistant), he put on special performances at schools.*

*'Phil was doing escape acts, getting free from being tied up by ropes, handcuffs, and even chains. On top of all that he was doing magic shows. After his performances, he asked the head teacher to donate all the admission money to charities. When his girlfriend gave up being his assistant, he decided to stop the school performances.*

*'Surprisingly Phil started playing chess. He became good at the game and entered into chess competitions. But it didn't have the 'buzz' that the magic tricks gave him. I told him: 'don't give up on your magic, get back into it again.'*

*And so it was, that after some time he did go back to entertaining the children as a magician, which he really enjoys. Since then, Phil has been doing numerous magic shows for the last twenty years; for seven of those years, I have been his assistant. His performances now include card tricks, magic hat, silks, and disappearing coins.*

*'Phil used to be called 'Phil the Magic Man,' but now it's 'Phil the Illusionist.' Every opportunity we get now to do shows for the children, we donate all the proceeds to charity, which to both of us is so important, especially when we know that the money its helping children with leukemia or going toward the upkeep of a children's hospice. I am proud of all my sons. They have all managed to succeed at what they set out to do, whether it be, magic, survival, music, or even computers. I'm proud of each one of them'.*

## Gosse, Philip Henry

Philip Henry Gosse (1810–1888) was born in the City of Worcester. A self-studied naturalist, he invented the institutional aquarium. In 1827, he sailed to Newfoundland, where he served as a clerk in the Carbonear premises of Slade, Elson and Co., where he spent much of his free time investigating natural history and he became a dedicated student of Newfoundland entomology.

Gosse returned to England in 1839, finding it hard to make a living. Fortune came his way when John Van Voorst, a leading publisher of naturalist books, agreed to publish his book 'Canadian Naturalist' in 1840. A dedicated religious man, in 1843, he wrote a 'An Introduction to Zoology' for the Society for Promoting Christian Knowledge (SPCK), he drew some of the illustrations, and writing this work inspired him to concentrate his studies of the flora and fauna of the seashore, and thereby starting a long career studying and writing about all areas of the natural world.

In 1844 Philip Henry Gosse sailed to Jamaica, spending two years in Jamaica specialising in the study of the country's birds. On his return to London in 1846, he continued to write, he wrote more than 40 books and 270 scientific and religious articles. He published a trilogy on the natural history of Jamaica including 'A Naturalist's Sojourn in Jamaica' in 1851. He became known as the father of Jamaican ornithology. For Christian companionship Gosse enjoyed the company of Moravian missionaries and their black converts, and he preached regularly to these Moravian congregations.

*Philip Henry Gosse and his son Edmund, photo 1857*

Gosse was a renowned Victorian naturalist but was above all a marine biologist, designing and popularising the aquarium, a word he invented. He found the term `Aquatic Vivarium' awkward and uncouth and coined the term `Aquarium'. Gosse was instrumental in the establishment of London Zoo's `Fish House', the first Aquarium at the Zoological Society of London.

## Green, Valentine

Valentine Green (1739–1813) was a solicitor in Evesham. He abandoned this legal profession and worked as a trainee engraver in Worcester. Later in 1775, he became an associate-engraver. In 1789, the Duke of Bavaria granted him the exclusive right of engraving and publishing plates from pictures in the Dusseldorf gallery. Green rose to the front rank of British engravers, a mezzotint engraver of exceptional skill.

## Walter de Grey

Walter de Grey, who died in 1255, was formerly King John's Chancellor. He became Bishop of Worcester in 1214, was a marked favourite with both Kings John and Henry III and was, beyond a doubt, the most distinguished English high-ranking member of the clergy of his time. He is said to have complied readily with all the wishes of King John and was certainly on the King's side during the great struggle for the Magna Carta.

## Gwilliam, Bill

Bill Gwilliam (1912–2002), a University lecturer, was a schoolteacher at both Christopher Whitehead School and Nunnery Wood Secondary School.

Bill was extremely interested in local history; he was President and a founder member of the Worcestershire Industrial Archaeology and Local History Society, founded in 1971. Bill wrote two books:

Old Worcester People and Places
Worcestershire's Hidden Past.

Bill Gwilliam appeared on both TV and Radio in 1998, and was awarded the MBE for his most remarkable work.

## Hardy, Robert and John

Robert and John Hardy migrated from Scotland to England and set up a business, Hardy & Co. in Worcester, in 1814.

Fifteen years later they were joined partnership with Richard Padmore; the company changing its name to Hardy and Padmore.

Hardy and Padmore's Worcester Foundry was a major English Foundry. Over the 155 years of trading they produced many fine castings including:

Worcester Bridge balustrade lanterns
Foregate Street railway bridge parapet
Dolphin Lamps on Westminster Embankment, London.
The Great Western Railway Bridge across Foregate Street.
The Fountain in Cripplegate Park.
The Clock opposite the Guildhall in High Street.
Manhole covers and drain grills of every size and shape were made and sent
    all over the world.
Traffic light control for Revo Electric.

Sadly the company went into voluntary liquidation in 1967.

## Harley, Robert Ian

Robert Harley (1953–2009) of Little Brookend Farm, Kempsey, grew up in the Barbourne area of the city. He was educated at the Saint Stephen's Church of England Primary School, winning a scholarship into King's School, Worcester. In 1977, he joined a newly formed business, Insight Surveys Ltd, pioneering in the use of CCTV and flow measurement surveys of sewerage systems. He eventually became co-owner.

In 1997, Insight Surveys Ltd, was acquired by South Staffordshire plc; but retained Robert as Managing Director.

In his private life, Robert Harley was generous, gregarious and popular, with that hugely infectious zest for life. He was well known as a sparkling raconteur and wit, and was a former President of the King's School Worcester old boys cricket club, the Old Vigornians CC. Robert was also a patron member of Worcester Rugby Club and a keen supporter of Worcester Warriors and Worcestershire Cricket Club.

Robert Harley was a passionate motorsport competitor, with a fine collection of classic and vintage cars. In 2006, he raced his 1929 Bentley at the '24 hour Le Mans.'

### Harper, Thomas

Thomas Harper Senior (1786–1853) a leading English Slide trumpet player of his day, was born in Worcester. At the age of ten he was sent to London to study the trumpet. It was there that he played with Eley's Royal East India Volunteers Band. He later taught trumpet at the Royal Academy of Music at the age of 40.

### Hastings, Sir Charles

Charles Hastings (1794–1866) was brought up at the Old Hall in Martley, attended the Royal Grammar School and witnessed a serious accident which resulted in his father becoming permanently incapacitated. This must have influenced his choice of career as he mixed with the medical profession at such an early age. Charles studied in under surgeons in Stourport, attended anatomy classes in London, and was elected house surgeon at Worcester Infirmary at the age of 18 years.

He continued his medical studies at Edinburgh before returning to Worcester, and the Infirmary, for the rest of his working life. As a prominent doctor, he fought for the lives of every cholera victim during each of Worcester's outbreaks, he was an authority on chest diseases,and wrote numerous scientific papers.

In 1832 Charles Hastings pioneered the formation of the Provincial Medical and Surgical Association, at a meeting on 19 July 1832, at the Board Room of the Worcester Infirmary it represented a major breakthrough. It grew and grew in numbers, and some twenty five years later became the British Medical Association (BMA) and the regulatory body the General Medical Council (GMC), as we know it today. He was knighted in 1850.

The road leading from Newtown Road to the Royal Hospital, was named Charles Hastings Way, in honour of Worcester's most famous medical son, who lived much of his life in Foregate Street. The BMA erected a memorial window to Sir Charles Hastings, in the north aisle of Worcester Cathedral. In 2012. Worcester University opened the transformed former Worcester General Infirmary as an establishment of higher education, naming it Charles Hastings Building.

*Blue plaque at Charles Hasting's Forgate Street home*

## Hick, Graeme, MBE

Graeme Ashley Hick, who played at New Road for Worcestershire County Cricket Club for 25 years, retired in 2008. For his services to the sport, Graeme Hick was presented with the MBE in the 2009 Birthday Honours List, by Her Majesty the Queen at an investiture at Buckingham Palace. The pavilion bearing his name was opened at the New Road cricket ground in May, 2009. He retired from at the end of the 2008 season to take up a coaching post at Malvern College.

## Hill, Thomas Rowley

Thomas Rowley Hill, the son of William Hill, co-founder of the Worcester vinegar firm of Hill, Evans & Company, carried on running the company with his partner Edward Bickerton Evans who was the son of Edward Evans, the other co-founder. He became Sheriff in 1857 and was Mayor of Worcester in 1858.

In 1865 Thomas Rowley Hill name was added to the Worcestershire Branch of Magistrates. 1874 He was elected a Member of Parliament for Worcestershire in the general election of 1874. He was twice married: his first wife was daughter of Richard Evans, and his second wife was the daughter of Edward Evans.

## Hollick, Robert, *Highwayman*

The Worcester Herald of March 18, 1820, reported the following news item:

*'Robert Hollick, was committed at the last Assizes for stopping and robbing on the highway in the parish of Claines, Thomas Gittins and Thomas Hawker, besides ill-treating the latter in a most cruel manner. This day he underwent the sentence of the law at the drop of our County Gaol. He was very penitent, acknowledged the justice of his sentence, and died with great resignation.*

*The execution was delayed by a very trying event – the unexpected appearance of Robert Hollick's aged mother, wife and child, and sister just as he was being led from his cell. He was asked by the chaplain whether he wished to see them, and had firmness enough to support the interview. To this he replied: 'I am firm.'*

*They consequently admitted: 'Nothing, however, could exceed the distress of the scene. This unhappy man only in the 22nd year of his age'*

## Hurdman, Edward

In 1621, Edward Hurdman became the first Mayor of the City. He was the second son of Thomas Hurdman of Napleton, Kempsey. He married his second wife Joan (a wealthy widow of Thomas Colley, brewer) in 1595, at Saint Andrews Church, Worcester. Edward Hurdman was buried in 1635; his widow Joan died two years later.

There are effigies of Edward Hurdman and his wife, on the sill of the south-west window of All Saints Church in Deansway. Hurdman's house was an imposing building close to the church, and he was churchwarden. He gave the church a communion cup which is still in use.

### Jarman, Rosemary Hawley

Rosemary Hawley Jarman was born in Worcester in 1935, she was educated at Saint Mary's Convent and then at The Alice Ottley School. A best-selling author both in the U.K. and the U.S.A., Rosemary left school, at eighteen, to study singing in London for the next three years, and developed a fine soprano voice. Family circumstances prevented her from continuing in this direction and she worked for a time in local government. She married David Jarman in 1958, and divorced amicably in 1970. She lived most of her time in Worcestershire at Callow End.

She began to write for pleasure, and followed an obsession with the character of King Richard III (1452–1485, who reigned 1483–85). With no plan to publish she completed a 228,000 word novel showing the King in his true colours, steering away from Tudor and Shakespearian propaganda. This work was taken up, almost accidentally, by an agent, and within six weeks a contract for publication and four other novels was signed with the publisher William Collins, (now Harper Collins). The first novel 'We Speak No Treason' was awarded The Silver Quill, a prestigious Author's Club Award, and sold out, within seven days, its first print of 30,000 copies.

Rosemary lived most of her time at Callow End. She lived with the author Roy T. Plumb for 18 years. They married in 2002, but the marriage was cut short when Roy died of cancer in 2003.

### Jeynes, William

William Jeynes owned a greengrocer shop at the bottom of Copenhagen Street, his son Robert often pushed a barrowload of greengrocery to Saint John's where he sold it. In 1923, William set up a shop for his son at 20 Pitmaston Road.

In the 1950s the family changed from selling greengrocery and moved to Tybridge Street where they opened a hardware shop, called Jeynes.

The grandson of William Jeynes, Bill (born 1940), William's grandson, decided to retire and closed down the hardware shop in August, 2011.

### Judge, Edward

Edward Judge (1906–1992), engineer and industrialist, was born in Worcester and educated at RGS Worcester. He studied engineering Saint John's College, Cambridge. He joined the steel manufacturing company Dorman Long in the north eat of England,

and became involved with the design and construction of Sydney Harbour Bridge and Tyne Bridge. He become Chief Engineer of Dorman Long; was made President of the British Iron and Steel Federation, overseeing the privatisation of the steel industry in 1967.

## Kay, William Kilbourne

There was a jeweller and watchmaker in Goose Lane (renamed Saint Swithin's Street during the 19th century). This shop still stands today, and is owned by a florist. It was once the home of John Skarratt, who was an apprentice clock and watch maker, founding his business here in 1794.

In 1814, Skarratt moved to number 2 Broad Street, where the premises were expanded. That shop still stands today and is called 'Shoe Zone.'

William Kilbourne Kay (born 1856, in Portsmouth) lived at number 10 Park Street, in 1881. When William got married to a school governess, Jessie Favendon, he was working for John Skarratt; living above the shop at number 2 Broad Street; and it was their that there first child was born.

Kay left the employ of Skarratt in 1886, and went into partnership with George Jones, an architect. They then started up their own jewellery and watch business in Foregate, which was called 'Kay, Jones & Co. of Worcester.' But by 1890, 'Kay & Jones' had dissolved. Kay, together with his three sons, changed the name of the business in Foregate, to 'Kay's of Worcester.'

The business was now a 'cash with order,' based on orders from customers who subscribed to the 'Kay's Catalogue.' William and his family were living at Wilberforce House, on the Ombersley Road.

In 1894, the business moved to Shrub Hill Road. In 1895, Kay's Universal Stores was registered at Company's House as Kay & Co. Ltd. William Kay retired 12 years later to Cheltenham, where he died in 1908. The business by this time had expanded and had established itself in the Tything, and there it remained for the next 94 years.

William Kay's sons, Tom, Edwin and Jack, were called up into the army, in World War I. More women were employed into the company because of the war that. After the war, Jack resigned his army commission and became a director of the company.

A plaque was unveiled at the shop in Saint Swithin's Street, by the wife of the chairman of 'Great Universal Stores Ltd,' where John Skarratt first started the business in 1794, eventually joining Kays in 1896.

In 1994, Kays celebrated its 200th anniversary.

## Kettlewell, Ruth

Ruth Kettlewell (1913–2007), actress, was born in Worcester, and was the second daughter of a clergyman. She was educated at Casterton School, and attended an art college. She married a curate at the age of 18, and played small parts in amateur dramatic productions. Ruth's husband died of scarlet fever, whilst serving as a wartime army padre. Ruth served in the Women's Land Army from 1942 to 1946.

By the late 1950s Ruth Kettlewell was securing small London West End roles. In 1959, she got her first film role in 'Room at the Top.'

In the 1960s Ruth's television career unfolded and she worked alongside the likes of Harry Worth, Joan Simms and Deryck Guyler. She played the Dean's wife in All Gas and Gaiters' and in 1966 had a small role in the seminal 'Cathy Come Home.'

Ruth Kettlewell was a devout Anglo-Catholic and an active member of the Actors' Church Union. She directed many amateur productions with a devotional theme for her church, which was Saint Augustine of Canterbury, Highgate, where she also served as churchwarden.

### Keogh, Brian

Brian Keogh (1926–2006) was born in Glasgow. During World War II Brian served with the Argyll and Sutherland Highlanders. At the end of the war he qualified as an accountant for Lea & Perrins.

In 1949, Brian married, and within three years had moved to Worcester. He lived there with his wife Mary and their three daughters.

Later, Brian Keogh become an archivist for the company. He wrote a book called 'The Secret Sauce' and probably referred to the notes that he found in a skip outside the Lea & Perrins factory in the 1980s.

Brian Keogh, who died in 2006, always said that he discovered the original recipe in two leather-bound folios written in sepia ink. The recipe was written in two different styles of handwriting, which analysts believe was due to the fact that no one knew the entire recipe. His daughter Bonnie Clifford has donated the papers to Worcester Museum.

### Kingsnorth, Paul

Paul Kingsnorth (born 1972) was born in Worcester, and attended the Royal Grammar School, High Wycombe (1985–1991). He studied modern history at Oxford University (1991–1994).

Kingsnorth was arrested during 'Operation Greenfly, a road protest movement at sites which included Twyford Down, Solsbury Hill, and the M11 link in East London. He worked in an orangutan rehabilitation centre in Borneo, and as a peace observer in the rebel Zapatista villages of Mexico. He was a sweeper of floors in McDonalds and an assistant Lock-keeper on the River Thames.

In 1999, Paul Kingsnorth was deputy editor of 'The Ecologist' for two years; and was named one of Britain's 'top ten troublemakers' by the New Statesman, in 2001. In 2004 he became co-founder of the Free West Papua Campaign, for the tribal people of occupied West Papua, and was made honorary member of the Lani tribe in 2001. Paul Kingsnorth worked on the 'comment desk' for the Independent; later he joined an environmental campaign group called 'Earth Action.'

## Lady in White

This very quiet lady roamed the streets of Worcester in the 1940s. She was dressed all in white with a white veil, and even her face was covered in white make-up. She came from Tunnel Hill. The story goes that she was jilted at the altar.

## Leader, Benjamin Williams

Benjamin Williams Leader (1831–1923), an English artist, was born in Worcester, the son of a civil engineer, Edward Leader Williams, a keen amateur artist, and a friend of John Constable; his mother, Sarah Whiting, was a Quaker. He was the first child of eleven children, and the family lived at Diglis House, which is now known as Diglis Hotel. He was educated at the Royal Grammar School, started a career in engineering, which he soon abandoned to study art at the Worcester School of Design where he learnt the skills of technical draughtsmanship. This apprenticeship along with his love of the Worcestershire countryside led him to submit a painting to the Royal Academy entitled 'Cottage Children Blowing Bubbles'. This was sold for £50 to a Philadelphia Collector much impressed by the talent of this young artist. He derived his artistic inspiration directly from nature and in particular his native countryside of Worcester, he painted mainly landscapes. He was very successful as an artist and was exhibiting his work at the Royal Academy in 1854, right up until his death in 1923.

In 1876, Benjamin married a fellow artist Mary Eastlake, they had six children. Leader was masterly at painting winter scenes, with bare trees, and an atmosphere of bleakness, and cold the viewer can almost feel. His most famous painting of this type is February Fill-Dyke (1881), now in Birmingham Art Gallery. By 1888 they had moved to Surrey where he lived for the rest of his life. Benjamin Williams Leader was made a Chevalier of the Legion of Honour on the recommendation of French artist Meissonier in 1889. In 1898, he was

*Severn Side, Sabrina's Stream at Kempsey on the River Severn*

made an associate ARA, and two years later, he at last became a Royal Academician (RA). His paintings were bought by King George V and William Gladstone, among others.

In 1914 he was made an Honorary Freeman of the City of Worcester, in recognition of his services as director of Royal Worcester Porcelain and a native of the city.

## Lewis, William

Alderman William Lewis is the only man to be elected three times as Mayor of Worcester (1844, 1845, and 1846). There is a portrait of William Lewis is in the Guildhall, painted by Soloman Cole.

## Lind, Jenny

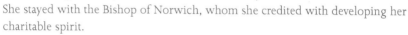

Jenny Lind (Johanna Maria Lind), (1820–1887) was not a Worcester girl, but I just have to mention her, because she lived her last years at Wynd's Point, a house, just behind the Little Malvern Priory, where she died from cancer. She was buried in the Great Malvern Cemetery. A chapel at the University of Worcester City Campus is named after her.

Jenny Lind was a Swedish opera singer, known as the 'Swedish Nightingale.' She began singing on stage at the age of ten. At the age of 17 years, she became a favourite in the Royal Swedish Opera.

In 1849, Jenny Lind performed at a concert in Norwich, organised by the Norwich Choral Society. She stayed with the Bishop of Norwich, whom she credited with developing her charitable spirit.

Jenny bought a house in Pottergate, Norwich; which was converted in 1854, reopening as a 20-bed Jenny Lind Infirmary for Sick Children.

## Littleton, Sir Thomas

Thomas de Littleton (1407–1481) was born at Frankley Manor House; and attended the Grammar School at Worcester. He became a barrister, in the Court of Common Pleas* in 1453, and was a judge in 1466. His tomb is in Worcester Cathedral.

*A common law court in the English legal system that covered 'common pleas'; actions between subject and subject, which did not concern the king.*

## Luff, Peter James, MP

Peter James Luff (1955), a Conservative Member of Parliament, was first elected as MP for Worcester in 1992 and then for the new Mid-Worcestershire seat in 1997.

## Maddox, Isaac

The appointment of Bishop Isaac Maddox (1697–1759) to Worcester in 1743, established a new development for the impoverished; and together with Doctor Wall, helped form the city's first infirmary, housing 30 patients, in Silver Street in 1746. It was one of only seven such places outside of London.

Bishop Maddox was a member of the Royal Society, and several of his letters promoted improvement of hospitals and criticised alcohol abuse.

## Mason, David Thomas

David Thomas Mason, from Worcester, born in 1946, is a legend in rock music history. A musician, singer, songwriter and guitarist, his musical talent was unashamedly bankrolled by his father Ted – or 'Choccy' as he was known in the family sweet shop, E. Masons, in Angel Place, Worcester.

Dave first found fame with rock band 'Traffic.' Throughout his career Dave has and recorded with many notable musicians, including: Jimi Hendrix, Michael Jackson, The Rolling Stones, Eric Clapton, and Mama Cass Elliot.

## Mason, Les

Group Captain Mike Logstaff, RAF station Commander, officially presented the DFM (Distinguished Flying Medal) to Les Mason in 2009. He won this medal 65 years ago in World War II.

Les aged 85 of Bath Road, Worcester, should have received it from King George V at Buckingham Palace, after the war, but the king was ill at the time; so Les Mason, received his DFM by King's Messenger at RAF Lindholme in Yorkshire, where he was serving.

Les Mason, was a Halifax bomber mid-upper gunner with 76 Squadron. He flew 33 missions in World War II, and took part in a very successful D-Day mission. He was a surviving member of Bomber Command; when almost half of the bomber crews failed to return from their missions. Les was quoted as saying that:

*'One of the first things you learned when you joined a bomber crew was not to make any close friends outside your crew. When you lost them it hurt too much.'*

## Minnis, Bethani

A tough test for 11-year-old Bethani Minnis, in 2008, was climbing to the top of Mount Snowdon, and she raised £1,075 for Noah's Ark Trust, the Worcester-based children's bereavement charity.

Bethani was spurred on to do this sponsored climb of 3,560ft, while studying at Saint Clement's CE Primary School in Henwick Road, where the children were taught about charity work. Bethani stated:

*'I enjoyed the climb very much although once we reached the clouds the climb got much harder and colder. Adam (Adam Newell, a retained firefighter who has travelled the world climbing mountains) asked if I was O.K. to continue, but there was no way that I would turn back until I had reached the top.'*

## Morris, William Richard, 1st Viscount Nuffield

William Richard Morris, 1st Viscount Nuffield, g.b.e. c..h. (1877–1963) was the founder of the Morris Motor Company. He was born at 47 Comer Gardens, west Worcester. When he was three years old his family moved to Oxford

On leaving school at the age of fifteen he became apprenticed to a bicycle repairer and seller; nine months later setting up his own business repairing bicycles from home.

The business was such a success that William Morris opened up a shop at 48 High Steer, Oxford. He manufactured bicycles as well as repaired them.

In 1901, William Morris designed the Morris Motor Cycle. Eleven years later he designed his first car, the 'Bullnose' Morris, and began manufacturing at a disused military training college which was in Cowley, Oxford. He was made a baronet in 1929, Baron Nuffield in 1934, and was made a Viscount in 1938.

## Nash, John

Alderman John Nash (1590–1662), Mayor, and twice representative of the City in Parliament during the reign of Charles 1. He was born into a wealthy family of clothiers, at a time when Worcester was the largest clothing manufacturing town in the country, employing 8,000 people, with 380 looms. The lengths of white cloth made in the City were called either Long Worcesters or short Worcesters, according to their length.

In his 72 years, Nash was a Roundhead Captain of Horse, a politician, a local administrator, and a successful merchant. He became a Justice of the Peace, and a Member of Parliament. Nash Passage, Worcester, is named after Nash's Almshouses, originally intended, like Saint Oswald's and Berkeley's for the aged, and to be known as Nash's Hospital. It still occupies the original site. He was also the founder of one of the Worcester charities, The Nash Hospital.

## Nash, Reverend Treadway Russell,

The Reverend Treadway Russell Nash, d.d. (1725–1811) was born in Clerkenleap, Worcestershire. He was educated at King's School at Worcester, and proceeded to Worcester College, Oxford. where he graduated with a Doctor of Divinity (DD).

Nash was the principal landowner at Bevere in the second half of the 18th century, living in Bevere House. Doctor Nash is more widely known as the author of his 'Collections for the History of Worcestershire' first published in 1781.

## Neathway, Tom

Paratrooper Corporal Tom Neathway, from Worcester, lost an arm and two legs in a roadside explosion in Afghanistan in July, 2008. and over many agonising months, the 25-year-old fought to walk again with the aid of artificial limbs.

It was through sheer determination that he climbed from his wheel chair to receive a campaign medal from Prince Charles in December, 2008. Corporal Tom Neathway was quoted in the press as saying at the time:

*'It has taken me two months of hard work. It probably should have taken longer…*

*My next goal will be to get back to work. It's no good being down in the dumps, I live the same life as I lived before, it's just that now I'm in a wheelchair.'*

## D'Oliveira, Basil

Basil Lewis D'Oliveira CBE (1931–2011), South African-born English cricketer, affectionately known as 'Dolly,' played 44 test matches for the English cricket team. He joined the Worcestershire County Cricket team in 1964, and in that the same year become a British citizen.

Basil D'Oliveira suffered with Parkinson's disease in later life, he died in England, aged 80, on 19 November 2011. A thanksgiving service, in Basil D'Oliveira's memory, was held at Worcester Cathedral on 28 Jan 2012. The veteran broadcaster, Sir Michael Parkinson, attended and was one of many who spoke in tribute, describing Basil D'Oliveira as a 'truly remarkable person.'

## Oswen, John

Worcester's first printer was John Oswen, in 1548. John came from Ipswich, Suffolk, where he was patronised by Cardinal Wolsey. He came to Worcester, having been appointed as official printer for the Marches, which included much of the Midlands.

Although he printed some 29 works, very few have been preserved.

John Oswen was a devout Protestant, and when Queen Mary, Catholic daughter of Henry VIII, came to the throne, Oswen's work ceased; his books proclaimed heretical; and those who possessed Oswen's books were ordered to give them to the authorities to be destroyed. Those failing to do so were classified as rebels and were executed; hence the reason for so few of John Oswen's books being preserved.

## Payne, Ernest

Ernest Payne was born in a cottage at 221 London Road in 1884. He took up a career as a carpenter. He borrowed his brother's cycle and was trained by his brother Walter, himself a successful racing cyclist, assisted by Arthur Hale, brother of another fine Worcester racing cyclist, Frederick Hale. Ernest's first race was in the summer of 1902 at Stourbridge. During his first season he raced in fourteen track events at a half and one mile, winning thirteen and coming second in the other. He joined the Saint Johns club

in 1903. By the end of June 1903,
Ernest Payne had already made a name
for himself, being referred to as 'the
Worcester Wonder' in the magazine
'The Cyclist'.

One of his major trophies was
the Challenge Cup, he won it outright
at the 1904 Whitsun meeting in Bath,
Somerset. He won more than 150
races including regional, national,
British Empire and Olympic
championships.

In the final of the Team pursuit
of the 1908 London Olympics, riding
with Ben Jones, C B Kingsbury and Leon Meredith, he led his team to victory with
superb pace-making over the last two laps. Ernest Payne led the team to a gold medal
victory with pace-making over the last two laps of the 1980 yards (1810 m) event.
They recorded 2 minutes 18.6 seconds, beating the silver medal-winning German
team by 10 seconds.

Retiring from cycling, he played football, in 1910, for Worcester Early Closers, and
later signed for Worcester City. He was in the team that won the Birmingham League in
1912. It's also reported, in a Worcester Saint John's Cycling Club memoir, that he made
first team appearances on the right wing for Newton Heath (later to become
Manchester United).

Ernest Payne died in 1961.

## Peach, Janet

On a chance meeting with Janet, during one of my daily walks with my German
Shepherd, Ellie, we chatted on a bench by the River Severn.

Janet is from Naunton Beauchamp, which is a very small village on the river Piddle,
nine miles from Worcester, and just over four miles from Pershore.

Janet told me the following story about the terrible floods of 1998:

*'It was mid-morning; and despite the torrential rain, I got into my old 'mini,' (Austin
Seven) and headed for Pershore, to the charity shop, where I worked part-time.*

*The rain got heavier. As I drove into the car park at the back, not visible from the shop,
I was horrified to see that the manhole covers were being pushed up by at least ten inches
of water. There I was in my wellies splashing my way across the car park to the charity
shop; there, I told my colleagues that I was going back home, because my
cat was shut in the downstairs part of the house, and suggested that we all lock up and
leave, before the flooding gets any deeper.*

*They wouldn't leave, but I did. I waded through the water into the car park, and thankful that the mini started okay. Travelling along Upton Snodsbury Road (B4082) in the pouring rain, was quite scary, having seen several cars abandoned, but I kept going. Half-way home, I had to stop, because the road was completely covered with water, it looked just like the sea.*

*I spoke to a nearby farmer who was sandbagging his front door. He offered to take me home on his tractor, then another tractor appeared and the tractor driver (who I knew) also offered to take me home, as he lived in the same village as me. So, abandoned the mini, and accepted his offer. As we turned right into Seaford Lane, we saw that the floodwater had turned into a raging torrent, I thanked the farmer, and waded into my cottage. My cat was terrified, I took him upstairs and laid him in a blanket on my bed.*

*The water was now two feet high in my living room and my feet were absolutely freezing. I rang the utilities; the Electricity company told me not to use the electricity; the gas board said it was okay to use the gas – good, I could have a cuppa!'*

*A neighbour, whose house was on higher ground, invited me in for a hot meal, which I accepted; her husband, however, had to abandon his car and walk home. He arrived soaked to the skin and freezing cold.*

*Later I rang the insurance people, who were quite prepared to rescue me, but not the cat (the catteries were full). I chose to stay with my cat. So there I was upstairs on the bed with my cat, who kept creeping up the bed and inspecting my face, I think he was just assuring himself that it was really me.*

*Lying there in my bedroom, I could hear a terrible rushing noise, which was coming from the nearby brook, it was in full spate.*

*The following day I went downstairs to inspect the place. The damage was awful, but at least the cat and I had survived the ordeal. The carpets, long curtains, and the furniture were ruined.*

*Then I discovered that all my water coloured paintings, which I had spent hours doing, had been destroyed by the flood. I was most distraught. I went upstairs and cried my heart out; I was so upset.*

*People I hardly knew, arrived at my house and offered their help. But the hardest part was yet to come; when I suddenly remembered the cupboards and found a lot of damaged food, etc.*

*I've no cat now, and as a widow, I still enjoy life. I am so grateful to charity shops. Nothing matches anymore; still I've got to like the mixed variety. What does it matter, I'm still here.*

*On a sad note, I discovered that the flood had washed away my poor fish from within their fishpond in the garden. And an even sadder story, was told to me, by the lady farmer, who lives opposite. She lost 50 lambs in waist-deep floodwater.*

*Friends in Evesham had some seven feet of floodwater and were rescued from their upstairs window balcony, by a helicopter.'*

## Pennethorne, Sir James

James Pennethorne (1801–1871) was born in Worcester. He became a notable architect, and was associated with several buildings and parks in central London.

James Pennethorne worked for Nash on a number of government buildings, and served for several years as chief architect at the Office of Works. He was awarded the R.I.B.A. (Royal Gold Medal) in 1865.

A few of the buildings Sir James undertook were:

*Regent's Park (started by Nash, was completed by Pennethorne after the death of Nash (1835).*

*Public Record Office, Chancery Lane, WC2 (1851–1858).*

*Ballroom at Buckingham Palace in 1854.*

*West Wing of Somerset House London, WC2.*


## Perrins, Charles William Dyson

Charles William Dyson Perrins (1864–1958) was born in Claines. He was the son of James Dyson Perrins, who was the owner of Lee & Perrins Worcestershire Sauce factory, the grandson of William Perrins, who was the co-originator of the Lea & Perrins secret recipe.

Charles was educated at Charterhouse School, and The Queen's College, Oxford; serving in the Highland Light Infantry. When his father died he took over the management of Lea & Perrins; he also took over his father's position as director of the Royal Worcester Porcelain Factory in 1891, becoming Chairman in 1901. He bought the company outright in 1934.

In 1946 Charles Perrins established the Perrins Trust in order to unite the factory museum collection and his private collection, securing their survival.

After his death his widow established the 'Dyson Perrins Museum' at the factory site, which is now known as 'The Museum of Worcester Porcelain.'


## Pitt, Ellen

Ellen Pitt of Hindlip, near Worcester, was killed at an aeroplane display in 1910, at the Herefordshire and Worcestershire Agricultural Show on Pitchcroft. There was great excitement during one of the first aeroplane displays ever witnessed in Worcester. Very few local people had ever seen a flying machine, and when its take-off was held up by a series of repairs and other problems, the crowd was tired and frustrated. When the aeroplane was ready to take off, the eagerness of some of the spectators had taken over from caution. She was one of a crowd of 14,000, who had surged forward on to the take-off strip, and was hit by an aeroplane; several other spectators who had surged over the safety ropes, suffered broken limbs.

## Redman, Bill

Bill Redman kept a lodging house in Quay Street in the 1950s. He was quite a character, driving around in his big flashy Ford Hudson American car called 'Tearaplane'. The house was a nightly haven, for tramps and buskers. One frequent visitor of the lodging house was 'Butt End Annie.'

## Runicles, Roy

Roy Runicles (1940–2008), member of the Salvation Army at Saint Richard's Hospice. He lived at Ambleside Drive, Warndon, with his wife Margaret. Roy was a talented player of the cornet, and will be especially remembered for his playing the 'last post' at Worcester Cathedral on Remembrance Sunday. Roy had worked at British Gas for 40 years, and was deputy bandmaster of the Salvation Army.

## Saint Wulfstan (Wulstan)

Wulfstan (1008–1095), educated at a monastic school in Evesham, was Worcester's very own saint. He became a deacon in 1033, then a priest; joining Bishop Britheah's 20-strong community of monks. In 1043. He was elected by the monks as their Prior and served them for twenty years. In 1084, Saint Wulfstan built the great Norman cathedral at Worcester.

Saint Wulfstan, lived a long life of devotion, and cared for the poor during those turbulent years of the 11th century. He served as Bishop of Worcester for 33 years up until his death. He was immediately declared a saint.

Saint Wulfstan's body was placed in a shrine in Worcester Cathedral, where thousands of mediaeval pilgrims came to pray.

*A stained glass window depicting Saint Wulfstan (Wulstan) at Worcester Cathedral*

## Sanders, John

It was during a visit to Tudor House in June, 2007, that I met John Sanders. John, born in 1932, was eight-years-of-age when he first came to Worcester. While showing me around the Tudor House he related the following story:

*'I've always been interested in the lifeboat service. I was a model-maker for many years, sailing my model lifeboats on County Hall lake. On one such day, a lady who ran the branch of the RNLI came up to see the lifeboats performing on the water. She asked if I could help the RNLI out with some model lifeboats.*

*'During 1986, I spent a lot of time on the east coast where I found like-minded guys who were also building model lifeboats. It just grew from there and I got involved with an expert model-maker, who was publicity officer for the Eastern Region of the RNLI. 'I worked with him, giving talks and showing model lifeboats, all along the east coast from Hunstanton down as far as Harwich.*

'I was spending an awful lot of time between my work as a Marine Motor Engineer and the RNLI (work always got in the way of my hobby). There I was up and down the east coast giving talks. My wife used to come with me. I'd leave her with lifeboat crews and their wives, and when I got back from a 'talk' there she would be cutting the sandwiches. Yes, we both really enjoyed it. Sadly my wife got cancer and died. I was heart-broken.

'Just after my loss, my friend, Margaret, who was running the RNLI branch, told me she was in desperate need of a full-time secretary. So in 1992, I became her secretary, continued for eight years and after that became a publicity officer, regional presenter, and in charge of demonstrations of lifeboats. It took up a lot of my time.

'Three years ago I had a stroke. Thus, I had to give up driving. But I'm still very much involved with the local branch as vice-chairman. A friend of mine had taken over as chairman, but wanted someone to back him up, and that was me. The Tudor House has become a continuation of my lifeboat involvement.

'In 1999, the local branch of the RNLI decided it would be good to have a fund-raising programme in Worcester. At that time this building was called The Museum of Local Life, and I was invited through a dear friend, Margaret Griffiths to put on an exhibition in the City of Worcester (in what we now called the 'tavern room'), to fund the RNLI.

'The lifeboat that I built especially for this exhibition in 1999, is upstairs. While I was building it, Margaret Griffiths said we should have the lifeboat that Worcester funded in 1869.

So that's what

I built. The idea being that at the end of the exhibition, if the curator wanted to keep it here, she could. But she didn't ask for it; so I gave it to Margaret Griffiths. When Margaret died in 2002, her sons gave it back, and I brought it here, to the Heritage Centre.

A scratch-built model begun by Morris Jones and completed by John Sanders. Another fine John Sanders achievement.

'It was through that exhibition, that I met the Curator, Nichol Burnett who was running the place for the Council. Yes, it was four years ago that we made this connection.

But the place at the time was falling apart and it needed a lot of restoration work done. So the council closed the place down.

'A lot of people were not happy about the place closing, people like John Bennet (who *is now our president). I thought to myself if the council cannot run the place how can a bunch of amateurs run it. It left a bad taste in my mouth – the way the council had ditched The Museum of Local Life – and I got to thinking if everybody thought like me it's never going to work.*

*'I decided to come down and meet some of the people working here voluntarily. After talking to them, I thought I'll volunteer too. And I've been coming here ever since. I still make models, the one that's waiting to go on display is HMS Worcester, which took me nine months to make. I also do repairs and I help Helen Wallis, who is house-manager here. I've built a World War I tank that was in Gheluvelt Park. I've got a Spitfire display that I want to complete, because the City bought two Spitfire in World War II. I'm also working on one of the Worcester City trams. I've got the chassis made already, but, because I've been in and out of hospital these last few weeks, I've had to slow down a bit. '*

At this point John turned to another volunteer worker nearby, John Kendrick, who had been a police officer in the 'Met.' and at Birmingham. Now retired he spends a lot of his time helping out at Tudor House. I was amazed to hear that there was a list of almost sixty volunteers, many of whom try to do at least one or maybe two days a week. John told me an incredible story:

*'HMS Worcester's ship's bell was returned to Worcester Guildhall. I went there to do the exhibition of lifeboats. Nichol Burnett, the curator here at Tudor House, asked me if I wanted some cabinets for my model ships because he had some upstairs, that I might be able to use. As I was, coming down the stairs of the museum, carrying a cabinet, I happened to pop my head round the open door of the storeroom, and there I spotted HMS Worcester's bell, which had been missing since the 1950s. Apparently after it had been put on display at the Guildhall for a while, somebody decided 'what the hell do we want that for' and it was brought to the museum and tucked away in this storeroom.*

*'When Nichol took over, she had no idea that the bell was on the premises, no idea at all. Suddenly everyone was asking about the bell. I was frightened to death because I knew that it had been missing, for the best part of 12 months I told nobody where it was.*

*'Then I was invited to the Dunkirk Veterans of Worcester, a disbanded unit. At the time I was chairman of the local Sea Cadets. And the V.R.W Destroyer Association were invited to the Dunkirk Veterans of Worcester, because they had been brought back from Dunkirk on HMS Worcester.*

*'The veterans were going to give Dunkirk memorabilia to the Sea Cadets. I was in the officers mess of the local territorials, when the subject came round to HMS Worcester. I said quietly, 'I know where the bell is.' Suddenly there was a deathly hush. An officer standing next to me said: 'What did you say?' I repeated. 'I know where the bell is.' After that the bell was taken back to its original resting place at the Guildhall.'*

Whilst walking around Tudor House, John told me about its involvement with the Cadbury's, he stated:

*'It was Richard Cadbury who put these stairs in at the museum. A mission hall that*

*was once further up the street, was funded by Cadbury. It was possibly because of the rationing during World War I, which was very extreme, that Richard Cadbury decided to get rid of this place, and it's highly probably that the whole scheme was a private venture of his anyway.*

*This room over the tavern is sometimes referred to as the 'ship room' because it is said to have ship's timbers. Ships had bendy bits of timber; it was the houses that had the straight pieces from the forest; and this was the difference in the oak used. An oak in the middle of a field spreads its branches, and this is where you get the curved pieces in the oak which ships used.'*

The following week I went to the Guildhall, to search out the Worcester Bell that John Sanders had mentioned. There I met 81-year-old Len (who has worked there for 25 years). He showed me to the Randall Room, which was formerly known as the Old Council Chamber (it was renamed in April, 1995, as a token of appreciation of the long and distinguished career of Councillor George Randall), and it was in this room that I found the HMS Worcester Bell which was dated 1922. I also discovered two plaques about the Spitfires. The first plaque reads as follows:

*'In 1940. The people of the City of Worcester gave £10,000 to the Government for the purchase of two fighter planes as an expression of confidence in victory in the war against Nazi Germany. Those two planes were named 'City of Worcester' and carried the coat of arms of the City.'*

A second plaque reads:

*In 1941 the Worcester Evening News and Times co-ordinated a 'Spitfire Fund' to which the citizens of Worcester donated £10,170. Two Spitfires were then presented to the Air Ministry, these being Mark II, as built at Castle Bromwich, with the serials P8045 and P8046, and known as City of Worcester I and II.*

*Worcester I flew with 72 Squadron in Northumberland, and successfully intercepted a German bomber attacking a convoy near Blyth. However on 2nd August, 1941 Worcester I was lost in a flying accident with 74 Squadron and its pilot, 21-year-old Pilot Officer Douglas Steven was killed.*

*Worcester II flew predominantly with 74 Squadron, but on 26th August, 1941 was on charge with 234 Squadron when attacking Maupertus (Cherbourg) Airfield, which was a German fighter base. Worcester II was hit by ground fire, and the pilot 24-year-old Sergeant Clifford Jacka, was killed.*

*This plaque is dedicated in memory of Pilot Officer Douglas Steven and Sergeant Clifford Jacka. We will remember them. Presented to the City of Worcester by the Malvern Spitfire Team. This plaque was unveiled on 13th may 1995, by former Warrant Officer Peter Fox of 234 Squadron, who was flying with Sergeant Jacka when he was killed, and in spirit of reconciliation, former Luftwaffe Lieutenant Hans Wulff EKI & II.'*

**Sandon, Henry** MBE

Mr Sandon, aged 79, was born in London in 1928, and came to Worcester in 1953, after training at the Guildhall School of Music. He was appointed music teacher at the Royal Grammar School and joined Worcester Cathedral Choir.

Henry Sandon developed a fascination with porcelain and china and in 1966 was appointed curator of the Dyson Perrins Museum and Porcelain in Severn Street, Worcester. He is a notable authority on Royal Worcester Porcelain, and made many appearances on the BBC's Antiques Roadshow.

Sandon's award of the MBE in the Queen's Birthday Honours in June 2008, came as a result of his services to broadcasting, charity and the ceramics industry. Henry is quoted as saying;

*'This is something really special. The British Empire is very dear to my heart. To be a member of it is really rather marvellous.'*


**Sandys, Martin**

Martin Sandys, of Ombersley Court, youngest son of Samuel Sandy, laid the foundation stone for Saint Swithun's Church in 1734.

He was a leading light in the rebuilding of Saint Nicholas Church he was the Town Clerk of Worcester.

Samuel Sandy (1695-1770) held the post of Chancellor of the Exchequer, leader of the House of Commons and Member of Parliament for Worcester.


**Scott, Sheila** OBE

Sheila Scott (1922–1988) was born Sheila Christine Hopkins. Sheila was born in Worcester, and educated at the Alice Ottley School. At one time she was married (1945–1950) to Rupert Bellamy. In 1943 Sheila started a career as an actress under the stage name of Sheila Scott, a name she kept.

In 1958 Sheila Scott learned to fly, and flew solo from Thruxton aerodrome, with just nine months training. She broke over 100 aviation records through her long distance flight endeavours, which included a 34,000 mile 'world and a half' flight in 1971. That was when she became the first person to fly over the North Pole in a small aircraft.

Sheila Scott was appointed an Officer of the Order of the British Empire (OBE) in 1968.

Sheila Scott's record breaking aircraft, which holds ninety world class light aviation records, was a single-engined Piper Comanche named Myth Too. It's on public display at the National Museum of Flight in Scotland.

## Shakespeare, Nicholas

Nicholas Shakespeare (1957) was born in Worcester, and educated at the Dragon Preparatory School, moving on to Winchester College and then Cambridge University.

Nicholas was a journalist for BBC television, he moved on to The Times newspaper, as assistant arts and literary editor. From 1988 to 1991, he was also literary editor for the Daily Telegraph and Sunday Telegraph. Nicholas wrote the following novels:

The Vision of Elena Silves (1989, Somerset Maughan Award, Betty Task Award).
The Dancer Upstairs (1995, American Library Association Award).
The Man Who Would Be King (1984).
Londoners (1986).
The High Flyer (1993).
Biography of Bruce Chatwin (1999).
Snowleg (2004).
Tasmania (2004).
Secrets of the Sea (2007).


## Sherriff, Alexander Clunes

A portrait of Alexander Clunes Sherriff (1816-1875) is in the foyer of the Guildhall. He was one of the most important Victorians in Worcester, a very prominent figure as both Alderman and Mayor of Worcester. He was a Member of Parliament for Worcester from 1868 to 1874.

Sherriff was brought to Worcester in the 1850s to rescue the Oxford Worcester & Wolverhampton Railway (OW&WR), which was so run down its customers nicknamed it the 'Old Worse & Worse'. Under Sherriff's leadership things improved so much that by 1863 it was sold to the Great Western Railway. He then formed the Worcester Engine Works Co. Limited with, amongst others, Walter Holland.

The Mayor's chain of office dates back to 1864, when it was commissioned by William Underwood and friends, who presented it to the Mayor, Alexander Clunes Sherriff as a personal gift. At the end of his term of office as Mayor, Sherriff presented this chain to the council (then called the corporation) 'to be worn by future Mayors of Worcester.' This chain of office is made of 18-carat gold (handiwork of Messrs Hugh & Roskell of London). The chain is so valuable that the insurers insist that the Mayor cannot wear it outside the Guildhall unless accompanied.


## Shuard, Ron

Ron Shuard (1935–2007) was a collector of postcards, and a leading philatelist. He was born in Rainbow Hill, and educated at the Saint Barnabas and Saint Stephen's schools. For thirty years he worked at James Ward Limited, an electrical firm. When this firm went into liquidation, Ron joined Heenan and Froude Limited doing electrical work. He finished his working life at Kays, on the maintenance team.

In 1988 Ron published his book 'Remembering Worcester,' about people and local scenes through decades. He married Janet in 1959, and they had five children, Carol, Alan, Robin, Susan and Philip.

## Siddons, Sarah
### A Legendary Actress

Sarah Siddons, born Sarah Kemble, made her stage debut in Worcester at the age of twelve in 1767. Her parents were a very prominent part of a touring company of actors. It was on the stage of a small barn theatre behind the King's Head Inn, in the High Street (opposite today's Guildhall). She played the part of Rosetta in a play called 'Love in a Village'.

During lengthy stays in the city Sarah Siddons was sent to a private girls' school in Thorneloe House (once part of the building of today's Eye Hospital in Barbourne).

Audiences truly admired her teenage beauty as did a fellow actor, William Siddons; they got married in 1773. Thus, at the age of only eighteen,

*Thomas Gainsborough, 1785*

Sarah bloomed into the legendary Mrs Siddons; making her debut on the London stage in 1775, as Portia in 'The Merchant of Venice.'

*Sarah Siddons as Euphrasia in The Grecian Daughter by Arthur Murphy, Theatre Royal in Drury Lane, 1782*

Overcome with nerves, Sarah's performance was a disaster, and after a provincial tour she returned to Worcester in 1779. But the following year she was called back to London and this time became an overwhelming success, establishing herself as: 'the first tragic actress now on the English stage.'

Mrs Siddon's stage career lasted over thirty years. Her portrait was painted by many artists including Sir T. Lawrence, Joshua Reynolds and Thomas Gainsborough. Her appearance at Drury Lane as Isabella in Southerne's 'Fatal `Marriage,' was a great triumph almost unequalled in the history of the English stage.

Mrs Siddon played Lady Macbeth, which was her greatest role, in 1785, holding her audience spellbound by the grandeur of her acting.

Sarah Siddon' died in 1831 at the age of 76 was mourned nationwide.

## Sleath, Robert

In 1788, Robert Sleath was a collector at the Turnpike Gate at the junction of Ombersley Road and Droitwich Road. He made George III, and all his retinue pay the toll when they came through Worcester. When Robert Sleath died in 1804, the following appeared in the paper:

*'On Wednesday last, old Robert Sleath*
*Passed thro' the turnpike gate of Death,*
*To him Death would no toll abate*
*Who stopped the king at Wor'ster -gate.'*

## Smith, Very Revd. Doctor William

William Smith (1711–1787) was born in Worcester. He was the son of the rector of Saint Nicholas' Church. He was educated at RGS Worcester, after which he went to New College, Oxford in 1728, where he stayed for several years gaining four degrees. He became headmaster of Brentwood School in 1748, then left to become vicar of Saint George's, Liverpool. In 1767, the Very Revd. Smith went to Chester, later moving in Holy Trinity, becoming Dean of Chester Cathedral.

Amongst the many achievements of the Very Revd. Doctor William Smith, was the translation of Tucydides' History of the Peloponnesian War.

## Snell, Hannah

Hannah Snell was born in Friars Street in 1723. Having been abandoned by her husband at the age of 22, after having lost her one-year-old child, she made her way to Coventry. There she enlisted as a young man, in the Duke of Northumberland's army. Later she deserted and joined the marines. She saw service in India, and fought at the siege of Pondicherry.

Hannah was wounded several time. On one occasion, when wounded in the groin, she maintained her secret by removing the bullet herself, as well as dressing the wound. R Walker wrote an account of her adventures in his book 'The Female Soldier' which caused quite a stir in London; the book was published in 1750. She appeared on the stage of Sadlers Wells. After all the publicity she decided to run a public house, which she named 'the Female Warrior.' The King granted her a pension of one shilling a day for life as an out-pensioner of Chelsea Hospital (where she is buried). She died in 1792, at the age of 69.

## Somers, John

John Somers (1651–1716) was born at Whiteladies, Claines, north side of Worcester, and educated the Worcester Cathedral school. Admitted into Trinity College, Oxford as a 'gentleman commoner', Somers studied law.

Admitted to the bar in 1676, he gained national reputation, in 1688, by assisting in the successful defence of the seven Anglican bishops who were brought to trial for rebellious incitement by the Roman Catholic King James II. After James was replaced by William of Orange (King William III) in 1689, Somers was elected to Parliament, and he became chairman of the committee that drew up the Bill of Rights. He was made Solicitor General, and by 1696 the King had appointed him chief minister and confidential adviser. In 1697 he was Lord High Chancellor of England, and was created a peer with the title of 1st Baron Somers of Evesham. John Somers was a leader of the group of influential Whigs known as the Junto from 1696 to 1716.

## Somerset, Edward

Edward Somerset, 2nd Marquess of Worcester (1602–1667), succeeded his father, Henry Somerset, 1st Marquess of Worcester. Edward was married twice, first to Elizabeth Dormer in 1628, with whom he had one son and two daughters:

*Henry Somerset, 3rd Marquess of Worcester, his heir and successor, became 1st Duke of Beaufort.*

*Lady Anne Somerset, who married Edward Winter, Knight, of Lidney, Gloucestershire.*

*Lady Elizabeth Somerset, who married William Herbert, 1st Marquess of Powis.*

## Stone, John

William Stone and his son John were maltsters in Worcester. They bought out a number of 'pubs' and after a number of years became well established. John Stone was always recognised in the street with his grand carriage drawn by a pair of grey horses; which became quite a familiar sight in the City.

## Thomas, Doctor William

Doctor William Thomas (1670–1738), grandson of Bishop Thomas, only son of John and Mary Thomas (daughter of Mr Bagnall of Worcester), was educated at Westminster School, moving on to Trinity College, Oxford. He took his master's degree in 1695, and in 1718, he took his doctor's degree.

In 1700, Doctor Thomas travelled to France, and then on to Italy, during which time he had mastered the French and Italian language; he also made himself master of the Saxon tongue. During this time he came to know Sir John Pakington.

Doctor William Thomas married Elizabeth, the only daughter of George Carter Esq. of Brill, Bucks. They had nine daughters and five sons. In 1721, with a view to the education of his children, Doctor Thomas came to Worcester. In 1723, where he met Bishop Hough to whom he dedicated the following:

'*Antiquitates Prioratus Majoris Malverne,*' 1725.

'*Dugdale's Warwickshire,*' 1730.

'*Survey of the Cathedral Church of Worcester and*

'*Account of the Bishops to AD 1660,*' 1736.

Doctor William Thomas is buried in the cloister of Worcester Cathedral, laying close by his grandfather, Bishop Thomas.

## Thomasson, George William

I was in Gheluvelt Park with my dog when I met another dog owner, Pamela Moran. We talked about Worcester, and her grandfather who died under very suspicious circumstances, Pamela wasn't too sure about the facts so I suggested that I might do some research on the case.

I discovered the following article taken from the Berrow's Worcester Journal, dated Saturday 23 September 1893

> *It is with a deep feeling of regret that we record the sad and untimely death of a member of the printing staff of this newspaper. On Saturday a body was found in the river and at once recovered to the mortuary. It has since been identified as that of Mr George W. Thomasson, who for nine years was employed at the Journal office.*

> *The hat and pipe of the deceased was found on a seat in Pitchcroft. Mr Thomasson was twice married, and leaves four children by his second wife, the youngest born only a fortnight ago.*
>
> *Mr Thomasson was an active man in Forestry. He had been chief Ranger of his court, the 'Robin Hood,' and was for some time secretary of the Juvenile Court.*
>
> *On Monday, September 18, 1893, at the Guildhall, Mr W. B. Hulme, City Coroner, opened the inquest. Edward Thomasson, Upper Tything, brother of the deceased, gave formal evidence of identification. The deceased he said, was 33 years of age, and was a printer employed at the Journal office.*
>
> *George Freeman, landlord of the 'Liverpool Vaults,' in the Shambles, said that the deceased had come into the Vaults shortly after 8 o'clock on Friday evening, he was perfectly sober. He had a pint of ale and a small bottle of beer. Still perfectly sober. On the Thursday evening the deceased told him he was in a little temporary difficulty, and wished he could meet with a friend from whom he could borrow a sovereign until Saturday night. He did not seem depressed in spirits.'*
>
> *'Tom Payter, a wheelwright, said that at a few minutes to six on Saturday morning he was on the towing path near the Cathedral. He saw a body of a man in the water.*

*Assistance was attained and the body was recovered. It was that of the deceased.*
*The body was about eight or nine feet from the bank. Frank Newman, a labourer,*
*who assisted getting the deceased out of the water, said the body was standing upright;*
*the feet stuck fast in mud.'*

*The witness noticed marks down the bank at the spot, as if someone had slipped into*
*the river. Robert Perks corroborated. P.C. Cook said that one shilling and five-and-a-*
*half-pence was found in deceased's pocket. William Ricketts, of the Dog and Duck Ferry,*
*found the deceased's hat and pipe on one of the seats on Pitchcroft on Saturday morning,*
*and on the same day Frederick Price, a sorter at the Post Office, found the deceased's*
*pocket-book containing papers, in the river near Diglis weir, about three yards from*
*the bank.*

*Thomas Banks, an engine driver, at the Journal office, said that he last saw deceased*
*at about six o'clock on Friday evening. He then told a witness he was going home.*
*Deceased was a man who was generally in good spirits.*

*Mrs Phaebe Smith, of Townsend Street, said deceased was her son-in-law. She saw him*
*last on Friday morning when he was about to start for work. He was then in excellent*
*spirits, as he always was. Witness did not think it likely that he would commit suicide.*
*Deceased came home very rarely the worse for drink. Deceased had no quarrel at home*
*and as far as witness knew, was in no trouble. When he left home on Friday morning*
*he had two postal orders for ten shillings each in his possession. He Said he would cash*
*them and be home early. Witness was not surprised at his non-arrival, as he was*
*frequently detained late at work.*

*P.C. Thomas said that he had examined the contents of the deceased's pocket-book.*
*He found nothing having any reference to deceased's death. The book chiefly contained*
*receipts, and a number of these related to payments to a loan office. Witness found no*
*receipts for money paid away on Friday. The postal orders were not among the papers.*

And so it was, that on Tuesday, 26 September, 1893, the jury, having attained no further
evidence, returned a verdict of 'found drowning'.

I visited Pamela and her husband Edward Moran and gave them this information.
Pamela told me the following story about her grandfather:

*'My Grandmother, who was George Thomasson's second wife, had four children.*
*My mother was the youngest of them, born two weeks before my grandad died.*
*When my mother was older, she was told that when my mother-in-law was old enough*
*to leave school she went to work for one year at the porcelain factory. There she made*
*friends with some of the workers that lived in a little cottage that was on a narrow*
*cobbled-stone street, which led down to the river.*

*They told my mother-in-law that on the night that all this happened they were awakened*
*by the clanking on the cobble stones of the wheels of a cart of some sort. They went to the*
*bedroom window and from there they saw a couple of gypsies pushing a handcart, which*
*was laden with something covered by a tarpaulin sheet.*

*That's all I was told. This has puzzled me all my life, I so wanted to know the truth. Unfortunately I never knew my grandmother, because she emigrated to New York. She tried to get my mother to go with her, but mother was terrified of the water. Father said he was born in England and that's where he's staying.*

*Grandmother came back to England just once, for a brief holiday when I was four-years-old. Every year my mother would take me and my two older brothers to the photographers in the Tything, so that she could send photos to my grandmother.*

*Auntie Ethel married Billy Pratley, that owned a china shop in the Shambles. Me and my cousin Sybil Norman, who was Billy's daughter, are the only two living on that side of the family. We had the shop at the end of this block for eight years, which the Co-op now have; our shop was called Moran's. We've lived here since 1989.'*

George William Thomasson (1860–1893) was a printer at the Journal office for nine years. He was an active man in Forestry, and worked as secretary at the juvenile court.

## Tyler, Jade
### Jade's Body Found
It was on the 10 January 2009, when the body of Jade, missing since 27 December 2008, was found in a field near the M5. Jade Tyler, was only 16-years-old and from Camforth Drive, Warndon.

On 30 January 2009, hundreds of mourners saw the horse-drawn carriage arrive at Saint Barnabas Church in Rainbow Hill, through the streets of Worcester.

Friends were reminded about Jade's active time as a Worcester News paper girl, and her love for football. She was buried wearing her Chelsea football shirt.

## Underwood, William
This Underwood dynasty has been in the Faithful City for over 160 years. The Underwood family firm was first in coal distribution and delivery but through five generations has expanded considerably into other areas: builders' merchants and steel stockholders, with bases in Worcester, Malvern and Hereford.

In 1852, William Underwood (1830–1890), came to Worcester at the age of 22 and worked as Superintendent of Goods, under Alexander Clunes Sherriff, the manager of the Oxford, Worcester and Wolverhampton Railway. Alexander Clunes Sherriff served as an MP, City alderman, and as Mayor in 1864.

The main freight traffic handled by the railway company at Worcester was coal, and A C Sherriff, realising a need for coal distribution to customers, set up the South Wales and Cannock Chase Coal and Coke Company in 1861; William Underwood left the railway and help Sherriff set up the company, he became its first manager and secretary.

William's son, **Frederick George Underwood**, at just 15, joined him at the coal company in 1867. Frederick later fell for Louise Emma Cridlan of a well-known Malvern family, and they were married at the town's Priory in 1879. He and is wife

Louise set up their home at 54 Rainbow Hill and Frederick stayed with the South Wales and Cannock Chase Coal and Coke Company for 23 years. He later set up his own business in 1890, as a coal merchant, trading as F. G. Underwood and Co., and was the very first to distribute coal around the city, under the logo of 'Underwood Coals.'

William Underwood died in 1890, at the age of 60, and not long afterwards when his son Frederick, just two years into his own business, died in 1892, at the age of only 40, leaving a wife and five children: two very young sons and three very young daughters.

With great courage, his widow took over the reins, helped by her brother, J. J. Cridlan and her father, John Cridlan. In 1896, a limited company was formed. In 1908, the Underwood Company offices had moved to 4 Foregate Street, expanding into number 6. For years thereafter the Underwoods was passed down and run by the younger generations of the family, it spread its wings, opened a builders' merchants depot in Pickersleigh Road, Malvern, acquired a steel stockholding business off Widemarsh Street in Hereford, and took over the large Vat House of the former Vinegar Works, off Lowesmoor for steel stockholding.

In 2000, the Tolladine Road builders' merchants centre was taken over by a West Country company, Bradfords, now known as Bradford Underwoods, the Underwood family retaining ownership of the land and property. Underwoods is now concentrating their activities primarily on property and steel stockholding.

## Vesta Tilley
### A Victorian Music Hall Star

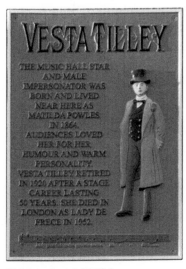

Vesta Tilley, born Matilda Alice Powles, (1864–1952) in Wyld's Lane, was the second of thirteen children. Her mother was Matilda Broughton and her father was William Henry Powles, he used the stage name of Harry Ball.

Vesta Tilley was only four-years-old when she made her first appearance on the stage. She first wore male clothes on stage when she was just five years old. Later she became bored with her song and impressions acts declaring: 'I felt that I could express myself better if I were dressed as a boy'. She impersonated dandies and fops and her dress was so immaculate that she became a fashion icon for men. Success quickly followed and by 1874 she had made her London debut at the Canterbury Hall. She made her first London appearance in 1874. She had a very long music hall career which extended throughout World War I.

*Birthplace plaque in Wyld's Lane*

Vesta Tilley was a great male impersonator, wearing 'top hat and tails.' She sang songs such as:

*'Following in Fathers Footsteps'*
*'Burlington Bertie'*
*'Jolly Good Luck to the Girl Who Loved a Sailor,'*
*which she sang on her ónal appearance at the*
*London Coliseum on June 5, 1920.*

Vesta Tilley spent 46 years on the stage and retired in 1920 with a special matinee performance. Nearly two million people signed the People's Tribute to her. She married Walter de Frece, who was active in theatre management and later became a Member of Parliament. On his knighthood, she became Lady de Frece. She died in Monte Carlo in 1952, at the age of 88. Worcestershire County Council has archived a collection of material that belonged to Vesta.

On Wednesday, May 13, 2009, the newly formed Vesta Tilley Society unveiled a plaque, to mark her birthplace. This plaque hangs over the former Garibaldi public house in Wyld's Lane.

## Turley, Jon

Jon Turley, born in Worcester in 1971, was a pupil at Royal Worcester Grammar School. In 1992, he enrolled at Cheltenham for a teaching degree which he completed over a four year period.

In 1996 Jon Turley taught at Cotwall End Primary School in Sedgley. Three years later he was teaching English at a private school in Dubai.

Returning to England in 2001, Jon Turley became a consultant with RM Computers. Jon's first book 'The Children are Revolting' was published in 2002, under the name of J.T. McQueen. His second book was called 'Empty Pages.'

## Sir Offley Wakeman

Sir Offley Wakeman, 3rd Baron Wakeman of Perdiswell (1850–1929). Perdiswell Hall was built for the Wakeman family in 1788. It was demolished in 1956. Thomas Wakeman who owned most of Claines, was mayor of Worcester in 1761.

## Walker, Lord Peter

Lord Peter Walker (1932–2010), was Worcester's MP for 31 years. When elected in March 1961 at the age of 29, he was the youngest MP in the House of Commons. His son, Robin was elected as Tory MP for Worcester in 2007.

Peter Walker is probably best remembered as the Energy Secretary during the 1984–85 miners' strike, when he presided over the defeat of Arthur Scargill. He retired as an MP in 1992. In that same year he was made Lord Walker of Worcester. He died at Saint Richard's Hospice after a long battle with cancer.

Margaret Thatcher, former Prime Minister, paid tribute to her former Cabinet minister, and is quoted as saying:

> 'Peter's long and distinguished career in Cabinet was ample demonstration of his effectiveness as a minister. He was thorough and determined … He always fought strongly for his beliefs. He was also one of the most persuasive communicators in government.'

The Right Hon. Peter Walker wrote a preface for the book 'City of Worcester' part of which reads:

> 'As secretary of State for the Environment I am naturally delighted that I shall have the privilege of representing a City set in such a fine environment as Worcester.
>
> Worcester is a City with a rich heritage of beautiful buildings and a City with the advantages of some of England's most green and pleasant land surrounding it.
>
> It is the blend of the diverse interests that make Worcester so fascinating, the old and the new, industry and agriculture, commerce and recreation, town and country…'

## Wall, John
### Martyred Catholic priest

John Wall was born, probably at Chingle Hall, near Preston in Lancashire, and educated at the English College of Douai, Belgium. He was ordained in Rome in 1648; in 1656 he came to work in Worcestershire. In 1678, he was apprehended under suspicion of being a party to the 'Titus Oates plot', a supposed Catholic conspiracy to kill King Charles II. He was sent to the Worcester jail, sent to trial, sent to London, he was brought back to Worcester and executed for being a Catholic priest and practicing Catholicism.

Saint John Wall was reputed to be the last Franciscan friar to be martyred in England. He was executed on Red Hill, Worcester on 27th August 1679.

A stained glass window, at Harvington Hall, depicting St John Wall and the secret chapel that he would have used with other priests in the times of persecution

## Wall, John

Doctor John Wall (1708–1776), a Doctor of Physic and very talented amateur painter, was born at Powick, young John was initially schooled at a small school in Leigh Sinton before becoming a pupil at King's School, Worcester.

In 1726, at the age of eighteen, John Wall obtained a scholarship at Worcester College, Oxford. Nine years later he obtained a fellowship of Merton College. He chose medicine as a profession, studying at both Oxford and Saint Thomas' Hospital. In 1836 he took his degree as M.A. and Bachelor of Physics.

In 1840, John Wall, now a Doctor, married Catherine, the daughter of Martin Sandys, Worcester Town Clerk. They had two sons, John and Martin, and three daughters, Catherine, Elizabeth and Mary. Doctor Wall's wife was cousin to Samuel Sandys, a Sitting Member of Parliament for the City of Worcester. He bought land in Foregate Street, where he built the house the family lived in and from which he practiced. So popular with patients, an estimated three quarters of the inhabitants of Worcester were reported to have been his patients, together with individuals as far afield as Ludlow, Stratford upon Avon and Alcester. Doctor John Wall gained a large measure of success and was the author of many medical papers.

He actively supported a campaign in 1745 to establish an Infirmary at Worcester, a building was purchased for £100 in Silver Street and an infirmary was established in 1746; John Wall was the first Treasurer and Martin Sandys a committee member of the hospital for many years, an effective father-in-law and son-in-law partnership sitting together discussing and planning for the hospital's future. When the Silver Street hospital outgrew its premises 2 acres of land were purchased for the sum of £200 in the Artichoke Field at the rear of Doctor Wall's Foregate Street home for the construction of a new infirmary. From the rear of his property, Doctor Wall would regularly walk over to check on the progress of the building work along what came to be known as 'Doctor Wall's Walk', and which is now known as Infirmary Walk.

Doctor Wall and William Davis, an apothecary who worked for the Silver Street Hospital, together with 13 other local businessmen, all shareholders, and instrumental in setting up the Tonquin Porcelain Manufactory at Warmstry House on the banks of the River Severn in 1751. He was very much involved in the porcelain industry, being an enthusiast in both chemical research and the artistic side. Doctor John Wall and William Davis are described as having 'invented and found out' the secrets of porcelain manufacture, and the period from 1751 to 1783 is referred to as the 'Wall Period'

He is understood to have spent the remaining 2 years of his life in Bath, although he retained his Foregate Street home.

## Walsh, Sir Richard

Sir Richard Walsh, High Sheriff of Worcester, and marksman, John Streete from Worcester, played a leading role in the capture of some plotters involved in the attempt to blow up the Houses of Parliament, or Gunpowder Plot, of the 5 November, 1605.

The High Sheriff arrived at Holbeache House in Staffordshire (owned by the Catholic Littleton family) with a posse on the morning of 8 November, surrounding the house. Refusing to surrender, the sheriff's men attacked. Streete killed Robert Catesby and Thomas Percy with one shot from his pistol.

Three other conspirators involved in the Plot were: Christopher (Kit) Wright, who was killed; John (Jack) Wright, who was mortally wounded and died; and Ambrose Rookwood, who was held at Worcester.

There were other plotters involved in the Gunpowder Plot, they were 'hung, drawn and quartered' at Red Hill, near the London Road, Worcester. They were: Humphrey Littleton, a prominent local landowner with Catholic sympathies, found guilty of harbouring traitors; John Witour; Father Oldcorne, who had been found hiding at Hindlip Hall; Ralph Ashley, also caught at Hindlip Hall; and Perkes, a tenant farmer.

## Walters, Marian

Marian Walters, born in 1942, started working at Kempsey Primary School, near Worcester, in 1976. She became school secretary in 1987, retiring in 2007, at the age of 65. Marian Walters was awarded the MBE, in June 2008, for her services to education and the arts. Mrs Walters was quoted as saying:

*'When I opened the letter I thought I had opened somebody else's post. I was totally shocked but very honoured. I keep thinking 'Why me?' There are so many people that do wonderful things.'*

## Ward, Kevin
### Editor Comes Home

On Monday 21 May 2007, Kevin Ward who was born in Worcester, and a former pupil of the Royal Grammar School, started his new job at Berrow's House, as the Editor of the Worcester News. Kevin, was 40 years-of-age, and married with two sons. Since 2005 he has been a publisher of a series of weekly newspapers, and prior to that was Deputy Editor of the Daily South Wales Argus newspaper.

Kevin Ward trained as a journalist at the Worcester News' sister paper, the Evesham Admag. Kevin Ward is quoted as saying:

*'I am delighted to be back in my home city and honoured to be Editor of the Worcester News and Berrow's Worcester Journal. My aim is to make our newspaper and website 'must-reads' for the people of Worcester and the surrounding towns ...*

*'I intend us to be in formative, fun, challenging, and interactive and campaigning ...*

*'Above all, I want us to be fighting on the side of our readers.'*

## Webb, Edward

In 1835, aged 27, Edward Webb bought for himself a horsehair weaving factory in Copenhagen Street. Next door to the factory was number 8, his dwelling house, built in 1733.

At the time the factory had only sixteen looms, but over the following ten years Webb was operating 29 looms. Dozens of poor children, working a ten-hour day, fetched and carried horsehair to the 100 weavers. But these children didn't go unnoticed. Edward Webb provided an evening school within the factory. The school was opened in 1846. and remained open for twenty-four years; over fifty children in attendance.

In 1854, steam power was introduced into the factory, (which at the time was called the Hair Cloth and Horsehair Carpet Manufactory). From 1925 to 1935, this very important carpet factory, now called Edward Webb and Sons Ltd, supplied plush floor coverings for cruise ships and railways throughout the world. It provided carpeting for Prime Minister Gladstone at number 10 Downing Street.

The factory also had the privilege of supplying 600 yards of 'Grey Worcester Carpet' for the 1893 Royal Wedding of the Duke of York (George V). It was the last of many carpet mills in the city. In 1935, the factory moved to the bottom of Newtown Road, on the corner of Sherriff Street.

Horsehair was also used for 'Interlinings', the stiffening material used in the lapels of jackets and coats. Edward Webb & Sons Ltd had a patented version known as 'Laptair' where the horsehair was laid lengthwise, wrapped with a thin strand of cotton, the cross-weave was all cotton. It was killed by a plastic substitute a few years later.

Edward Webb became Mayor of Worcester in 1847, and was a strong supporter of the Health of Towns Act led by Doctor Charles Hastings.

## Wesley, John

John Wesley (1703–1791) along with his brother Charles are credited with founding the Methodist movement in this country. John was the fifteenth child of Samuel and Susanna Wesley (there was nineteen in all, but only seven lived). At the age of five John, was rescued from a burning rectory, which left a deep impression on him throughout his life. He was deeply entrenched with the Church of England, especially as his father Samuel Wesley was rector at Epworth.

John Wesley travelled many miles on horseback, often preaching three times a day. He is thought to have preached more than 40,000 sermons.

He was first recorded to visit Worcester in 1760. He visited again nine years later and preached in the 'Riding House'. A chapel was built in New Street in 1772 which was opened by Wesley himself. He stayed with John and Anne Knapp at the White House in Lowesmoor.

There are quite a number of entries in his journal relating to Worcestershire, and the society of Worcester. One such entry on Sunday, March 21, 1784, reads:

*'I preached to a crowded audience in Saint Andrew's church. The Vicar read prayers, and afterwards told me, 'I should be welcome to the use of his church, whenever I came to Worcester.'*

## Whiby, Bosel A

Tatfrith, a monk of Whiby (Whitby) Abbey, was nominated for bishop, but he died before consecration, and Bosel, one of his fellow monks, was consecrated in his place. He became the Bishop of the Hwicce, or the first Bishop of Worcester, in 680–691AD. He founded the Royal Grammar School around 685AD.

## White, James

James White (1775–1820), son of Samuel and Mary White, was born in Worcester and baptised at the Church of St. John in Bedwardine.

He was the author of 'Falstaff's Letters, and was a lifelong friend of Charles Lamb, the great English essayist. White was founder of the first advertising agency in 1800, which moved to 33 Fleet Street, London, and became R F White & Son Ltd. James White is the great-great-grandfather of the author T H White (1906–1964).

## Wilding, Michael

Michael Wilding (1942) was born in Worcester. he was educated at the Royal Grammar School, winning a scholarship to Lincoln College, Oxford. Michael is an author and professor of English and Australian Literature at the University of Sydney, and a founder of the Australian publishing Company Wild & Woolley.

Michael Wilding is internationally renowned for his many short stories and literary criticism. he also has entries in the Oxford Dictionary of Australian Literature and also in The Cambridge Guide to Literature in English.

## Williams, Edward Leader

Edward Leader Williams (1828–1910) was born and raised in Worcester and he lived at Diglis House, now Diglis Hotel, the son of a civil engineer and amateur artist, also called Edward. His brother, Benjamin Williams Leader (1831–1923) was an artist, and would often accompany his father's great friend, John Constable, on sketching trips along the River Severn. After attending the Royal Grammar School Worcester, Edward Leader Williams junior became an apprentice to his father.

As a civil engineer, he is well-remembered as the chief designer and chief engineer of the Manchester Ship Canal during its construction. The canal opened in 1894, described as 'a feat without precedent in modern history'. Edward Leader Williams was knighted by Queen Victoria on 2 July 1894, after its opening. He was also the Vice-President, Institute of Civil Engineers.

## Winsmore, William

William Winsmore, born in 1739, was a Mayor of Worcester. During that time, he was having an affair with the daughter of a wealthy widower, an Archdeacon. The following year the daughter who was only 18, eloped with William Winsmore, and they got married in Edinburgh. After nine months of marriage, the wife left Winsmore. She died of smallpox less than one year later. Their daughter was looked after by William's sister, Lucy.

Meanwhile, William Winsmore, became Sheriff of Monmouth in 1766. William Winsmore was involved in the development of the canals, losing a large fortune. His daughter married Aunt Lucy's son, Doctor Thomas Hooper, who owned property at the Cross, at the back of Saint Nicholas Church, in Worcester.

## Wood, Mrs Henry

Mrs Henry Wood was born Ellen Price at Number 18 Sidbury in 1814. Her father was Thomas Price, a glove manufacturer. She married Henry Wood, head of a banking firm in India, at Whittington Church.

Some years later Ellen, having returned to Worcester because of illness, she started writing novels, which included:

| | |
|---|---|
| Mildred Arkell. | Johnny Ludlow. |
| Mrs Halliburton's Troubles. | East Lynne. |
| The Channings. | |

Most of her novels depicted life in Worcester, with characters from real life. Her most popular novel was 'East Lynne' which was first published in serial form in a magazine in 1861.

## Woodbine Willie

The Revd. Geoffrey Anketell Studdert Kennedy, born the son of a vicar in an impoverished and overcrowded industrial area of Leeds, in 1883. After reading divinity and classics at Trinity College, Dublin, he graduated and began teaching. He soon realised that he wanted to follow his father into the clergy; he became a vicar, first in Rugby and then in Worcester in early 1914. He chose the poorest parish, Saint Paul's in the area known as Blockhouse Fields, on the south side of City Walls Road. He became known for the fire and passion of his sermons, and was renowned for his passionate approach to Christianity.

Revd. Studdert Kennedy was an army chaplain during World War I. He was posted to Rouen in France, which was a staging point for those on their way to the front line. Troops in their hundreds got off the trains in the railway sidings for a breath of fresh air and to enjoy the luxury of the canteens nearby. It was in the canteens that the Revd. Studdert Kennedy mixed with the lads to raise their spirits. He got them to sing three particular songs:

'Mother Machree' for husbands

'Little Grey Home in the West' and

'The sunshine of Your Smile' for lovers.

During this time he began writing poetry that was as passionate as his sermons. Revd. Studdert Kennedy would deliver a powerful christian message in just a few words.

As the troops boarded their trains again, the Reverend would walk up and down

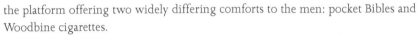

the platform offering two widely differing comforts to the men: pocket Bibles and Woodbine cigarettes.

He witnessed for himself the horrors of the trenches in World War I. Here is one short verse of a poem that he wrote:

'Waste of Blood, and waste of Tears,

Waste of youth's most precious years,

waste of ways the Saints have trod,

Waste of Glory, Waste of God –

War!'

Revd. Geoffrey returned at the end of the war, awarded the Military Cross in 1917 for action under fire, he was now a national figure, he had served in the front line with the troops with only his two knapsacks, one containing pocket Bibles and the other containing cigarettes.

The Revd. Geoffrey was invited to Buckingham Palace where he was asked to preach to George V. The king was so impressed that he appointed Kennedy as Royal Chaplain.

Geoffrey, his wife and their three children, lived in a house in Bromyard Road, and for the next seven years he was kept very busy on tours. One day, in the spring of 1929, whilst preaching at Liverpool the Rev. Geoffrey developed a flu, which turned into pneumonia, and in a matter of hours he was dead.

He now rests in peace at Saint John's Cemetery. At his funeral about 2,000 people lined the streets, some throwing Woodbines packets onto the passing cortege. His life and work is commemorated with a plaque in Worcester Cathedral, and the Social Services Building in Spring Gardens named 'The Studdert Kennedy Centre' is a living memorial to his love of the city.

### Wyatt, George Harry VC

George Harry Wyatt (1886–1964) was awarded the VC for gallantry in the face of the enemy. He was 27 years old, and a Lance-Corporal in the 3rd Battalion, Coldstream Guards in World War I.

Whilst in battle in 1914, at Landrecies, France, Wyatt's battalion was engaged close to some farm buildings when the enemy set alight straw sacks in the farmyard. Lance-Corporal Wyatt dashed out under very heavy gunfire from the enemy only 25 yards away, and extinguished the burning straw, making it possible to hold the position.

Later, although wounded in the head, he still continued firing until he was unable to see owing to the blood pouring down his face. A medical officer bound up his wound and ordered him to the rear, but Lance-Corporal Wyatt returned to the firing line and went on fighting. Later he was to achieve the rank of Lance-Sergeant.

### Yarnold, William

William Yarnold (1857–1905) had been serving in South Africa, while his wife back home was having an affair. She left the marital home to live with her lover. On his return home, Yarnold tracked down his wife and tried to persuade her to come home. When he failed to change her mind, he pulled out an army knife and stabbed her in the back, severing her spinal cord.

William Yarnold was 48 years-old when he was hanged in Worcester on 5 December 1905 by the famous Henry Pierrepoint, a former butcher's apprentice from Nottingham, turned hangman in the late 1890s. He was appointed executioner in 1901, and over the following nine years hanged 105 people.

### Yelland, John

Former University of Worcester Chair of Governors, John Yelland, received an Honorary Masters degree and a University Fellowship In 2007. This was in recognition of his many contributions to the University of Worcester. He became the founding president of its new College of Fellows and he was chairman of the governors helping the University of Worcester gain university status.

In 2009, John Yelland received the OBE in the Queen's Birthday Honours List, for his voluntary service to the community. John Yelland has been very active over the past 30 years in developing Worcester's Arts and Heritage organisations. He formed a group that helped save the Huntingdon Hall from being turned into a car park.

# Chapter six
# Historical titbits

## Ale – That Good Old Pint!

Ale is a type of beer that is brewed from malted barley using a top-fermented brewers' yeast, that ferments the beer quickly. Ale was first created by the Babylonians almost 5,000 years ago.

Here is just a few of Worcester Brewers:

Earnest Watkins, Brewer, operated from New Street, Worcester; it ceased brewing in 1939.
Speckley Brothers, Ltd, in Barbourne Road, bought Stallard's Britannia Brewery in 1884.
Lewis Clarkes Brewery, Angel Place, Worcester was founded in 1869.
Robert Allen, Mumford & Co (Barbourne Brewery) was formed in 1900.

## Archeological Dig

During the preparatory stages of constructing a new £60million Library and History Centre at The Butts, a ten-week community excavation and public programme, called 'The Butts Dig' took place from 4 August to 12 October 2008. Groups who actively took part in, or visited the dig included: primary, secondary and special schools and local children's clubs, Lifestyles, Worcester Task Force, MotoV8, University of Worcester undergraduate archaeology students, the Young Archaeologists Club, University of the Third Age, Worcester Archaeology

Society, and Natural England staff. There were 90 volunteers who registered to work alongside the professionals from Worcestershire Historic Environment and Archaeology Service. With their trowels they unearthed well-preserved coins, including a Charles II coin of 1672, brooches and bracelets, huge numbers of sherds of pottery, and almost complete vessels such as a beehive. The dig revealed floors and foundations of Roman buildings and a Roman road confirming that the site was a 'hive' of activity from the late 1st century to the mid-4th century with at least four phases of occupation. Large drainage and boundary ditches by cobbled roads and yards were discovered, and by at least three buildings, the first range of complete Roman buildings seen in Worcester which were probably the houses of urban craftsmen. A total of more than 3,000 visitors were given tours of the excavations and exhibition rooms.

## Barber – shop sign of the past

Did you know that the old-fashioned barbershop sign (the red and white striped pole) comes from the days when the barber acted as a surgeon. In the past the barber would extract teeth and often 'bleed' people on purpose to cure maladies. Thus the red stripe on the barber's pole was representing blood; while the corresponding white stripes represented the bandages.

In 1758, a barber was put in the stocks for a day, at the bottom of Mealcheapen Street, just for shaving customers on Sundays. However, those who came to see him in the stocks, had a heart, because they threw him pennies and halfpennies, and he earned more from his punishment than he did through several days working at the shop.

## Beer, Cider & Perry Festival

The annual CAMRA-run (Campaign for Real Ale) event, which started in 1999, takes place on the Worcester Pitchcroft Racecourse, for three days in August. It is organised by Bill Ottaway, and it grows more successful each year. In 2012 visitors were spoilt for choice with more than 230 real ales and over 130 perries and ciders. About 13,250 drinkers sank more than 46,000 pints inside a 3,500 square metre marquee on Pitchcroft.

## Clothiers Company

On the 10 June 2008 the Prince of Wales and the Duchess of Cornwall visited the Commandery and presented The High Master of the Worcester Clothiers Company, Andrew Grant, and its 35 members, with a purse which contained £453.15. Prince Charles was quoted as saying at the time:

*'It seems that the good people of Worcester, or at least the members of the Clothiers Company, have a long memory in particular as far as unpaid debts are concerned. By long, I mean nearly 400 years.'*

The debt was incurred by King Charles II in 1651, when he commissioned the Worcester Clothiers Company to make uniforms for his troops; promising to pay after the battle of Worcester. But Cromwell defeated the army and the King fled to Europe, leaving the bill unpaid.

Prince Charles was given a receipt by Mr Grant and his members, who were dressed in their red tunics and black gowns (made especially for the occasion, by the tailors, Armstrongs of Worcester), who pledged to remember the occasion every year as Settlement Day. This was marked with a bottle of 1948 Port and a toast to 'The Clothiers Company and that year of 1651.'

## Constables or Watchmen

In the days before Sir Robert Peel introduced the 'police force,' the city of Worcester employed Constables (watchmen) in order to protect citizens and their property.

When weather was bad, each constable had his very own shelter (very much like a sentry box), which was wheeled into position when they came on duty. At night, it was not unusual for constables to remain in their boxes rather than stay on 'the beat,' with the consequence of often falling asleep.

In those early days of the 19th century, one of the favourite pastimes of the young tear-a-ways, was to carry the sleeping constable in his box some distance away, and on one occasion, depositing the box to the side of stream, so that when the poor fellow woke up he stepped into the stream, getting drenched.

It was after that episode that the boxes were securely chained up in their specific place. By 1597 the city had eight 'night watches' consisting of men equipped with clubs.

In 1833, Worcester formed its first police force with thirteen paid 'Watchmen and Constables.' As the force grew, it opened up three police stations, the first was in Union Street, followed by another in Copenhagen Street. The old police cell block still survives in the Guildhall.

*Worcester's police in the 1890s*

The City's first police patrol car arrived in 1930.

## Faithful Overalls Factory

Worcester-based company, Faithful Workwear, and until 2009 had its home was in Northwick Road, a family business established in the 19th Century owned by former Tory cabinet minister Stephen Dorrell MP, a member of the Russell and Dorrell family. The company made industrial clothing, and in the summer of 2009 went into 'pre-pack administration', vacated the factory and the building was later demolished.

The site of the old Faithful factory has now been redeveloped, controversially, as Eastbank Court, a purpose-built Extra Care Scheme offering retirement accommodation.

*Above: Faithful Overalls factory before demolition*

*Below: An architect's plan drawing for a new factory on the Nortwick Road site, dated 1938*

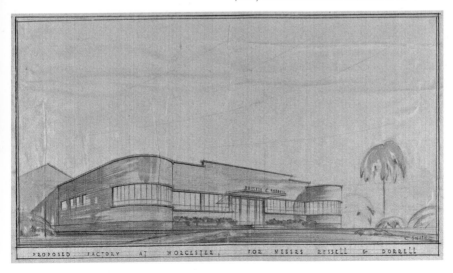

## Heenan & Froude

Worcester Engineering firm, Heenan & Froude, constructed the Blackpool Tower. This 518ft high structure was built between 1892 and 1894 using over 2,000 tons of steel. In its heyday, Heenan and Froude factory, at Shrub Hill, employed 2,000 people. Though, it no longer exists, its name will forever be remembered.

## Movement Gallery

WICVEWENT
MOVEMENT
MOVEMENT
**MOVEMENT**

A very small art gallery was opened in October, 2010, in an old public toilet, on Platform Two of Foregate Street Railway Station. The Movement Gallery is only 35sqm, it opened with its debut show, 'The Ultimate Painting', featuring epic landscapes by New York painter Jacob Feige. The gallery plans to hold at least four exhibitions a year.

## Oak Apple Day

Royal Oak Day, or Restoration Day, marks the restoration of England's monarchy and celebrates our freedom from tyranny. It is part of our English culture and heritage. This special public holiday of 29 May was first celebrated in the wake of the triumphant return of Charles II to London after nine years exile in France. This day was not only announcing the restoration of the monarchy, welcoming back

Britain's monarchy after the period of Cromwell's republic, but it was also Charles II's birthday. 29 May was named Royal Oak Day over 350 years ago by Act of Parliament. Worcester people are encouraged to raise a flagon to Oak Apple Day every year on 29 May, a tradition that has been carried out in Worcester since 1660.

The Chelsea Pensioners wear an oak leaf which reminds them of the story of how, with the help of the Pendrill family at Boscobel House, Charles II hid in an oak tree; he escaped with his life by hiding in the 'Boscobel Oak' when he was defeated at the Battle of Worcester in 1651. They wear light red-coloured uniforms in the summer months, and warmer blue uniforms are worn in the winter months. These uniforms, which they have to wear when walking outside the hospital, date back to 18th century. They also have a special scarlet uniform together with a three-cornered hat for ceremonial occasions, such as Founders Day, or Oak Apple Day.

## Peregrine Falcons Settle in Worcester

In April, 2007, a pair of peregrine falcons set up home at one of Worcester's best known landmarks, the top of Saint Andrew's Church Spire, off Deansway. This came to be a very special occasion, because these birds usually use coastal cliffs. But now they had come into the big cities, such as London, Birmingham, Manchester and Cardiff; so we in Worcester were very privileged to see them. The pair successfully hatched a young falcon which fled the nest in July;

it returned the following year. Peregrine falcons are the fastest living creature on the planet. They can dive at speeds of over 200mph. Surprisingly the female is a third larger than her partner; taking on bigger targets for food.

## Saint Richard's Hospice

Saint Richard's Hospice offers a free service caring for patients and families in Worcestershire who are living with the threat of life-threatening illnesses.

It was founded in Droitwich in 1984, operating from the home of a local GP, Dr Jenny Bulman. It takes its name from Richard de la Wych who was born in Droitwich in 1197 and was declared a Saint in 1262.

Originally founded as Saint Richard's Hospice at Home, in 1985 it merged with the Good Shepherd Hospice Group from Malvern when the name changed to the Saint Richard's Hospice Foundation. In 1985 the Hospice moved to Castle Street, Worcester.

In 2004, services continued to grow, and to meet demand, the hospice started a £5.25m appeal to build a new centre with the first, and urgently-needed, specialist palliative care 'In-patient Unit for South Worcestershire'. In 2006 the new Saint Richard's Hospice opened in Wildwood Drive, Worcester.

It is an independent Worcestershire charity and each year it gives care and support to around 2,200 patients and family members, helping them towards the best quality of life possible.

Saint Richard's Hospice mission statement reads:

### 'Caring for Life'

*Saint Richard's Hospice exists to enhance, through specialist palliative care and education, the quality of life of patients and those important to them, suffering from cancer or other life-threatening illness.*

## McNaught & Co Ltd, The Tything

One of the most successful companies, virtually unknown today, was McNaught and Co. which had large showrooms, workshops and stables in the Tything on the corner of Saint Mary's Street.

Started in the 1790s by Mr J. A. Mcnaught, a highly skilled craftsman, he started building horse drawn traps and light carriages for the local gentry but graduated into the larger vehicle market.

By 1862, the business had grown rapidly and was now called McNaught & Co Ltd., exhibiting its vehicles in their own Park Lane showrooms in London, and in international exhibitions all around the world, winning many Gold Medal awards. These included London 1862, Paris 1867, Philidelphia 1876, Paris 1878, Sydney 1879, Melbourne 1880, Calcutta 1884 and an Inventions exhibition 1885.

As well as the Lord Mayor of London's Coach they built carriages for the Metropolitan and County Sherrifs, H.R.H. the Prince of Wales, and the Duke of Conaught. They had the showrooms in Park Lane and in Birmingham as well as a superb showroom and galleries in Worcester.

The company employed the finest painters and gilders, lining and decorating with ornate heraldic coats of arms on to the superb coaches built in fine oak, ash, walnut, hickory, elm, birch, and mahogany woods. A considerable harness department produced award winning tackle using the finest leathers produced in the Worcester tanneries.

### Three Choirs Festival

The Three Choirs Festival dates back to the 18th century and falls in Worcester every three years. It is the oldest music festival in Europe and takes place between the cathedral cities of Worcester, Gloucester and Hereford.

### Hill, Evans & Co. vinegar works

It was William Hill and Edward Evans who, in 1830, founded their vinegar works on Pheasant Street. Purchasing a six-acre site at Lowesmoor, they built a factory in 1852, where they produced some of the finest vinegar in England.

The vinegar works closed in 1965, and was occupied by a number of small factories. This very impressive vinegar factory (which became known as the 'Great Filling Hall') still stands today as a grade two listed building.

The Vinci Construction UK, has converted this 158-year-old Great Filling Hall into a permanent home for:

*The 214 (Worcestershire) Battery Royal Artillery (Volunteers), or Territorial Army Centre.*

On 28 September 2012, Prince Edward unveiled a plaque at the centre, now called Dancox House. It has plenty to offer: a well-equipped gym, state-of-the-art classrooms and meeting rooms, and a large hall suitable for lectures, conferences, exhibitions or social events.

*Above: Faithful Overalls factory before demolition*

*Below: An architect's plan drawing for a new factory on the Nortwick Road site, dated 1938*

### Worcester Artillery Volunteers

The Artillery Volunteers set up their first Battery in Worcester in 1865. At first the soldiers only had wooden mock-up guns to display. Later the volunteers were presented with a headquarters building at Southfield Street.

There was also the Worcestershire Militia, who were called up once a year, for a couple of weeks, for annual training. These men were billeted in the inns of the city, and it was the duty of these licensee's to provide a accommodation, until their barracks were built at Norton.

The Militia trained on Flag Meadow. It must have been a wonderful sight to see as many as a thousand men in their scarlet uniforms, marching every week through the main streets of the city.

# Worcester Festival

The Worcester Festival first started in 2003 as three weeks of events, activities and fun for everyone. It is an opportunity for local people to attend and participate in a wide selection of professional and community events and activities. The Festival is for the people of Worcester and the surrounding communities, and is a series of partnerships between large cross sections of the community creating a huge range of activities.

The Worcester Festival is not a music festival, it is not an arts festival, but it does feature both, it is simply a festival for every generation to enjoy. People of all ages, from all walks of life just get together and have a good time together.

The Festival starts on a different date each year, but it always ends on August Bank Holiday Monday, going out with a bang with a most splendid fireworks display. Every three years the Festival runs for an extra week to incorporate the Three Choirs Festival, an annual week-long classical music event that rotates between the cities of Hereford, Gloucester and Worcester.

## Worcester Heritage & Amenity Trust

This Trust is made up of a group of enthusiastic volunteers who have a passion for Worcester's history and heritage. Based at Tudor House which has had a varied life in the five centuries since it was built. It has been used as a work place for weavers, clothiers, tailors, bakers, painters and brewers. It was used as lodgings, the Cross Keys Inn, Cadbury's Tudor Coffee House, an air raid wardens' post and billet office, a school clinic and | a museum. The Trust opened its doors in May 2004 and works to keep the building available to the public as the Tudor House Heritage & Education Centre. Displays of local history, crafts and culture over several rooms are complemented by a shop and coffee room serving drinks and cakes.

W.H.A.T. is dedicated to keeping open public access to Tudor House for the all the citizens and visitors to Worcester.

## Worcestershire Film Festival

The county's first ever celebration of film was held at The Hive over the first weekend of November in 2012. Starting with an opening gala night on Friday 2 November, continuing all through Saturday and Sunday, the Festival showed 30 films from local filmmakers, with special screenings of feature-length films and Q&A sessions with the directors and filmmakers themselves,. Industry professionals gave fascinating workshop sessions.

## Worcester Music Festival

Created from a desire to bring together and showcase the city's burgeoning musical talent, Worcester Music Festival was launched in 2008 by 'Not Just Sauce' promoter Chris Bennion and has been growing every year since.

Worcester Music Festival is a non-profit making event, run by an enthusiastic team of 25-plus volunteers, largely local musicians or people associated with the Worcester music scene. Not only does it provide a showcase for local musical talent, but it provides education and professional development opportunities through a variety of workshops and masterclasses.

Each year, the festival supports a local charity and, since 2008, over £25,000 has been raised.

## Worcester Victorian Christmas Fayre

Worcester hosts the leading Victorian-themed street market in the midlands over four days at the end of November. Coaches full of visitors flood into the city, from far and wide, to sample a first taste of Christmas. Started in 1992, the Fayre fills the streets with over 130 stalls, music and theatre, stallholders and visitors dressing up in period costume, embracing the Victorian Christmas spirit.

**Worcester volunteer and artist**
*Louise Draper RIP, Gheluvelt Park*
'In memory of a local artist'

Life cannot always stay the same
just learn and live each day
the very best that you know how.

05–02–76
02–05–11

# Chapter seven
## Places around Worcester

Within a radius of thirty miles around Worcester you can enjoy the beauty of the countryside, known as 'the English Vales'. The thatched houses are just one feature of the Worcestershire landscape. There is a vast variety of interesting places to visit:

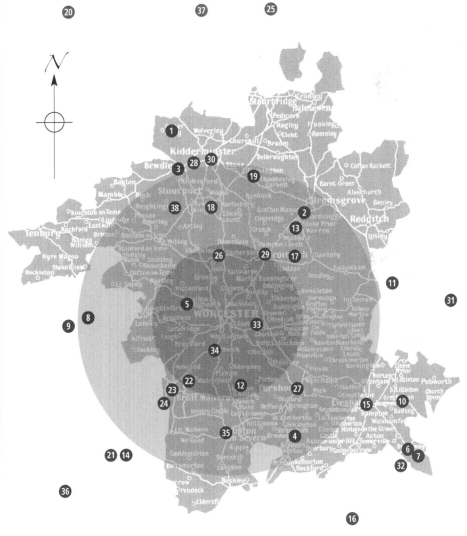

## 1. Arley Arboretum

A very old privately-owned arboretum and park, containing a listed walled garden, an Italianate garden, and a tea-room.

## 2. Avoncroft Museum of Historic Buildings

On the open-air site spanning seven centuries as a public display of 27 restored historical buildings, and working windmill. Buildings have been rescued from being destroyed, and very carefully rebuilt on this 15-acre site in Stoke Heath, Bromsgrove.

## 3. Bewdley

A Georgian town, with Bewdley Bridge, over the River Severn, built by Thomas Telford in 1798.

## 4. Bredon Hill

On a clear day, one can see ten counties from the top of Bredon Hill. In the village is a 14th century mediaeval tithe barn, built of Cotswold stone, entrusted to the National Trust.

## 5. Broadheath

Sir Edward Elgar's birthplace at Crown East Lane, Lower Broadheath, is a pretty little cottage. The Elgar Birthplace Museum and Visitor Centre has been built alongside the cottage.

## 6. Broadway

Broadway is the gateway to the Cotswolds. There is also a folly built around 1760, called the Tower, which was once home to William Morris, founder of the Arts and Crafts movement.

## 7. Broadway's Fish Hill Folly

A 55ft high 18th century Gothic folly, which is at the top of the infamous Fish Hill, is on the A44. Its the second highest point in the Cotswolds. On a good day you can even see the Black Mountains.

## 8. Brockhampton Estate, Bringsty, Herefordshire

Beautiful 1,700 acre farming estate was bequeathed to the National Trust in 1946.

## 9. Bromyard, Herefordshire

This delightful market town, steeped in history, sits amongst some of the most scenic countryside in England, by the River Frome.

## 10. The Fleece Inn, Bretforton

Originally built as a longhouse in the time of Chaucer. Lola Taplin lived her entire life at The Fleece Inn, Bretforton. She died in 1977 aged 83 years, having run the inn on her own for the last thirty years of her life. She bequeathed the inn to The National Trust making it the first pub in the country to be owned by the charity.

## ⑪ Coughton Court, Warwickshire

Coughton Court, in the care of the National Trust, has been the home of the Throckmorton family since 1409. It holds a unique place in English history associated with hiding fleeing Catholics in the time of Henry VIII, and its close connections to the Gunpowder Plot of 1605.

## ⑫ Croome Park & Court

A park landscaped by Lancelot 'Capability' Brown in 1751 with a mid-18th century Neo-Palladian mansion also designed by Brown and some of the internal rooms designed by Robert Adam. Croome Park was requisitioned by the RAF, becoming RAF Defford Aerodrome. Wellington bombers were based there. After the war, Croome was restored into a very beautiful park, with the help of the National Trust.

## ⑬ Droitwich Transmitting Station

The large broadcasting station aerials between Droitwich and Bromsgrove are a prominent feature on the Worcestershire landscape. This station is the BBC's most powerful longwave transmitter. The Radio 4 LW signal from Droitwich is by far the strongest in the UK, covering most of England and Wales, the Benelux, parts of West Germany (covering the areas where the British Forces in Germany are based) and Northern France. Built in 1934, it is owned and operated by Arqiva, formed by National Grid Wireless.

## ⑭ Eastnor Castle, Eastnor, Ledbury

A beautiful fairytale castle in the foothills of The Malverns, private home of the Harvey-Bathurst family, was designed by John First Earl Somers in 1812. It is set in an area of outstanding beauty, with delightful woodland walks.

## ⑮ Evesham

Riverside market town of Evesham is situated in the centre of the famous horticultural Vale of Evesham – the fruit and vegetable basket of England.

## ⑯ Gloucester Steam Railway

*The Friendly Line in the Cotswolds*

This award-winning railway, is run entirely by qualified volunteers. It runs from Toddington to Winchcombe and then on to Cheltenham Race Course. I went on a Sunday train excursion from Toddington to Cheltenham, pulled by a handsome engine called the Black Prince. Wonderful.

## ⑰ Hanbury Hall

A William and Mary-style country house, set in 400 acres of parkland and gardens, built in 1701, in local red brick, by Thomas Vernon, a lawyer and whig MP for Worcester. Now under the wing of the National Trust.

## ⑱ Hartlebury Castle, Worcestershire County Museum

It was King Burghred of the West Mercians who, in 850, gave the land on which Hartlebury Castle now stands on, to the Bishops of Worcester, for whom it has been home for over a thousand years. During the Civil War in 1644 the Commissioners for Array, being pursued, fled to the castle (built in the 13th century as a fortified manor house) from Ombersley, believing it to be a safe haven. During occupation of the Royalists a mint was set up at the castle; and a minted rare coin (half-crown) is now on display at the County Museum.

## ⑲ Harvington Hall

Three miles away from Hartlebury Castle is Harvington Hall, most of which was built by Humphrey Pakington around 1580. He inherited the hall in 1578, and began turning the mediaeval building into a Tudor manor house. The walls were covered with paintings and tapestries; and glass windows added to add light to the rooms.

The building was encased with limestone and red brick. Priest hides were added, which had become necessary after Queen Elizabeth's law of 1585, which banned Catholic priests from entering the country. Hop Pocket Craft Centre, Bishops Frome

## ⑳ Ironbridge, Shropshire

Ironbridge sits beside the River Severn, but a little further afield at 40 miles from Worcester. It has had lots of famous visitors, including Benjamin Disraeli, 1st Earl of Beaconsfield.

In 2003, even the Queen and Duke of Edinburgh walked across the bridge. The Ironbridge Gorge Museum is worth a visit with its thirty-five historical sites within the Ironbridge Gorge World Heritage Site, which includes ten museums.

## ㉑ Ledbury

Sixteen miles from Worcester is the town of Ledbury. It has many black and white timber-famed buildings. In 1645, the Royalists fought Cromwell's army in the main street. The Royalists won that battle.

## ㉒ Madresfield Court

This stately home is the seat of the Lygon family, and is linked to Evelyn Waugh's novel, Brideshead Revisited. The Great Hall we see today was built in the 12th century. The house was rebuilt in 1593; and modernised as a Elizabethan moated home in the 19th century. The chapel designed by Philip Charles Hardwick, is quite stunning.

## ㉓ Malvern

Malvern was a spa town for the Victorians, and has been famous for its bottled water since 1622. Great Malvern is almost a thousand years old, and was developed around a 11th century priory which has the finest collection of mediaeval stained glass windows in the country.

## 24 Malvern Hills

A trip round the beautiful Malvern hills is a must. They look out over a landscape that sums up the whole of rural England. These hills are the true boundary between England and Wales.

From the Worcestershire Beacon (the highest point at 1,3995 ft) one will see the imposing domes and pinnacles of the Welsh hills to the Wye Valley and the Black Mountains of Brecon.

## 25 Moseley Old Hall

This lovely old building south of the M54 near Wolverhampton. This was where King Charles II hid during the fight against the Parliamentary army, led by Oliver Cromwell in 1651. Charles was hiding in a priest hole, when the soldiers searched the place.

## 26 Ombersley

This charming village, once owned by Evesham Abbey, has half-timbered Elizabethan and Jacobean houses lining Main Road. The Crown and Sandys, a Grade II-listed building, in Hill Top Lane, was once a 17th century coaching inn. It was named after Lord Sandys of Ombersley Court.

The King's Head, in Main Road, dates back to the 15th century; King Charles is said to have rested here after the Battle of Worcester.

## 27 Pershore

This pretty little town virtually grew around Saint Oswald Abbey, which was founded in 689. The church lantern tower dates from 1350. Pershore Abbey, which was one of the largest in the country, was destroyed during the Reformation, Pershore is quite famous for its plum orchards, and calls itself the 'capital of the plum.' The town itself has a six-arched bridge across the River Avon, which dates back to the mediaeval period.

## 28 Safari Park

The West Midlands Safari & Leisure Park is at Spring Grove, Bewdley, just 16 miles from Worcester (A499). The park was established in 1970, and has a four-mile safari trail.

## 29 Salt Way

A great British track, the Worcestershire Salt Way, extends for miles from Droitwich where the salt industry had carried on from the days of the Roman occupation. The Covercroft Works was just one of several works in Droitwich, but was the only one that had its own railway system.

## 30 Severn Valley Steam Railway

The SVR railway was in the transportation period from 1862 until 1963. Since 1970 it's been involved in the tourist industry. and run by unpaid volunteers. It provides sixteen miles of beautiful countryside, between Kidderminster and Bridgnorth in Shropshire.

## ③① Stratford-on-Avon

Close to the Shakespeare Centre, Henley Street, there is also Anne Hathaway's Cottage and Mary Arden's Farm.

## ③② Snowhill Manor, Gloucestershire

The land of Snowshill Manor was owned by Winchcombe Abbey as early as 821, until the Dissolution of the Monasteries in 1539. It is a fascinating tudor mansion that was purchased in 1919 by Charles Padget Wade, an eccentric architect and antiquary. It is currently a National Trust property that houses his superb collection of treasured objects of craftsmanship and design collected throughout his life.

## ③③ Spetchley Park Gardens

This park, three miles from Worcester is a 30-acre Victorian paradise. It's been home of the Berkeleys since 1606. Elgar spent time here, where he wrote his masterpiece: 'Dream of Gerontius.'

## ③④ Stanbrook Abbey, Callow End

It was in 1623, when the Benedictine nunnery for English ladies was founded at Cambrai, France. During the French Revolution, 22 nuns were imprisoned in Compiégne for 18 months. In 1835 the survivors came to Callow End, destitute. Stanbrook Abbey was then established when the Benedictine nuns bought the original Georgian house called Stanbrook Hall.

## ③⑤ Upton-Upon-Severn

An attractive riverside town with its famous annual, summer Upton Jazz Festival and Upton Blues Festival.

## ③⑥ Westons Cider

In the heart of the Herefordshire countryside, Westons Cider Mill is situated in the old village of Much Marcle, on the road between Ledbury and Ross-on-Wye. In 1878 Mr Henry Weston came to farm at The Bounds, a farmhouse nestled amongst apple and perry pear orchards. Two years later he joined the Herefordshire cider-making community and began a legacy of tradition and quality.

Visitors of all ages can discover the secrets of traditional cider making by joining one of the daily guided mill tours, enjoy a tasting session and take home a free gift.

## ③⑦ The White Ladies Priory, Boscobel

The White Ladies Priory, now in ruins, was one of the first houses for religious woman in England. The name is reference to the white habits of Augustinian Canonesses of the 12th century. Among the many sisters that found happiness at the White Ladies Priory was the mother of Saint Wulstan.

## ③⑧ Witley Court and Gardens

A site of ruins of one of England's great country houses built in 1655, and the beautiful Persus and Andromeda fountains (once the largest fountains in Europe) which have been beautifully restored.

The largest fountain at Witley Court representing Perseus and Andromeda, designed by William Nesfield in 1857, took three years to build and is carved from Portland stone. It was made to rival anything Italian designers could produce. It is thought to be the largest fountain in Europe, its figures are based on Greek legend. The water which spouts from the sea monster's mouth reaches a height of 36 metres. The fountain has been gloriously restored by the Poseidon Fountain Restoration Society, bringing back to life the 120 separate jets hidden amongst giant shells, sea nymphs, dolphins and the monstrous serpent.

# Notes